DO YOU
WANT A MIRACLE?

MIRACLES, MATERIALISM, ANGELS
AND OTHER SPIRITUALITIES

DO YOU WANT A MIRACLE?

MIRACLES, MATERIALISM, ANGELS
AND OTHER SPIRITUALITIES

WILLIE HUGHES

MERCIER PRESS
WHAT YOU NEED TO READ

MERCIER PRESS
Douglas Village, Cork
www. mercierpress. ie

Trade enquiries to CMD Distribution
55A Spruce Avenue, Stillorgan Industrial Park,
Blackrock, County Dublin

© Willie Hughes, 2008

ISBN: 978 1 85635 575 9

10 9 8 7 6 5 4 3 2 1

A CIP record for this title is available from the British Library

The Scripture quotations contained herein are from the New Revised Standard
Version (NRSV) Bible, © 1989 by the Division of Christian Education of the
National Council of the Churches of Christ in the U.S.A., and are used by
permission. All rights reserved.

Mercier Press receives financial assistance from the Arts Council/An
Chomhairle Ealaíon

Printed and bound by J.H. Haynes & Co. Ltd, Sparkford

For those who have tasted
the bitter fruit of despair in life,
May they find in this compact little book,
the loving hand of hope.

Never be overcome. Overcome!

To the Three Wise Men

Ӡԑ CONTENTS Ӡԑ

❧ PREFACE ❧

The aim of this book is to help us develop spiritual awareness. Each chapter concentrates on one topic; first provid-
ing a theoretical background and then presenting a practical two-step programme. The first topic, 'Miracles', begins with a discussion of miracles, their purpose, spiritual
significance and their accessibility today, and out of this
comes a set of practical steps to implement the theory and
obtain a miracle. Similarly, the other topics, 'Materialism',
'Forgiveness', 'Peace', 'Angels' and 'Death', present a practical programme that springs from a theoretical discussion.
Each of the six topics provokes a response that involves
our emotions, intellect and spirit. What is presented is an
ideal; it is up to each of us to find his or her level and to see
what works in practice.

This book has an individualistic perspective. We live
in an age of individual responsibility where nothing is accepted simply on the authority of others. In the recent past,
christian spirituality was presented in a more utilitarian
way: people were encouraged to follow a course of action
in which the primary goal was the welfare of others. All
too often, this led to the individual seeing their needs as
secondary to the needs of others. Today we tend to feel
that we cannot give to others that which we do not possess
ourselves. For instance, we are unlikely to bring happiness
to others if we are unhappy. However, the individualistic

perspective of this book is entirely consistent with the christian approach. Jesus constantly encouraged people to follow him, not out of adherence to religious law, but as a result of their inner commitment.

The spirituality presented in this book is based on christianity, one of many spiritual traditions that offer theoretical and practical guidance on spiritual development. It is intended to encourage those who were born into christianity to experiment to achieve spiritual awareness. In addition, it appeals to those who were born into the christian tradition but no longer feel that christianity has meaning for them; it challenges them to look again at their tradition and to test its propositions in an objective way. Equally, this book may be of interest to people of different spiritual persuasions who feel they may benefit from exposure to other spiritual paths.

No matter who the reader, this book promises that with real and balanced determination, all spiritual aspirations will invariably be rewarded.

For more information, please do visit my website: www.doyouwantamiracle.com

Willie Hughes

∞ **1** ∞

MIRACLES

To doubt is the greatest insult to the Divinity

Padre Pio

❧ INTRODUCTION ❧

Many of us fervently want miracles in our lives. We may not frame it in that way but, essentially, that is what we are looking for. From a christian standpoint, nothing could be more theologically sound than asking Jesus for the grace of a miracle. So why is it that we so seldom wholeheartedly approach him with our requests? It would seem that somewhere along the line we have, firstly, lost the understanding of the nature of divine intervention, and secondly, lost the practice of asking for it. We have distanced ourselves from the rawness of boldly asking Jesus to intervene in our personal lives and grant us what we dearly desire. However, this is what Jesus constantly looked for when he interacted with his disciples and others.

Today we have to examine anew the relationship between Jesus and miracles and with the clarity of insight, courageously stir ourselves to ask for miracles.

MIRACLES

The importance of miracles is that they build trust in Jesus. In the gospels, when Jesus performed a miracle, people tended to be filled with a desire to follow him and to learn more about what he had to say; such dramatic interventions in their own practical lives made them feel drawn to trust him. Jesus encouraged this trust for he wanted to lead them out of their narrow experience of life, dominated by suffering, to a life infused with peace. Thus, for Jesus, miracles were primarily a means of rewarding and encouraging trust. Over time and experience this trust led to a general faith in all he had to say about life and the nature of God's love.

Today, we live in a world where our daily experience reinforces the notion that life is nothing more than what we can see and touch. It is therefore very difficult for us to move from this material and sensory world to the non-material spiritual world. However, when Jesus intervenes in our material world and, through miracles, dramatically helps us, then our hearts are filled with gratitude and wonder. We are greatly inspired to trust him and listen to what he has to say about spiritual reality. If we learn to trust him in the material world, it is a smaller step to trust what he says about the spiritual world. We have a genuine reason to follow him because we have seen how impressive he has been in the world we know and how he has reached out to us in an objectively verifiable way. He has been willing to do this for us; therefore he is worth listening to when he talks of other unseen things.

Throughout the gospels, Jesus is constantly performing miracles. Miracles are central to his way of leading people on, of encouraging them to trust and develop their faith. Nowhere does a miracle occur where trust is not present. The two elements are intrinsically linked. Jesus could have granted miracles to everyone and anyone, friend and foe alike – after all, this would have attracted greater crowds and even impressed his detractors – but he did not. Instead, Jesus used miracles to encourage those who showed trust to stretch themselves, to take greater risks and benefit from doing so. The stronger the trust, the happier Jesus was. He is often seen pushing people hard to deepen their trust that a miracle is possible. Sometimes people might have to ask several times before he grants the miracle; he seems almost to ignore them until he is satisfied with their commitment. Jesus is compassionate but he does not interfere with our free will. In the end he leaves it up to us; we have to stir ourselves. For this reason, he is often a tough taskmaster. Miracles are not for the faint-hearted. They both encourage and reward those who boldly reach out their hand in trust to him.

This then is the challenge to us today if we are serious about requesting miracles: we have to go deep into our hearts and learn to trust Jesus.

Requesting Miracles Today

We have largely lost confidence that Jesus will grant miracles to those who trust him today. We need to believe again in our hearts that Jesus earnestly wants to reward and encourage our trust and will grant us miracles. We have to learn again how to ask for miracles. We have to learn how to have confidence and how to display it.

What will follow in the next section is a simple programme to help us achieve a state where we feel confident and comfortable in asking Jesus to intervene directly, in a most verifiable way, in our personal lives. It will help us to request miracles.

The programme suggested has, as its basis, some of the miracles Jesus performed, as recorded in St Matthew's Gospel. These miracles are reproduced at the end of this chapter. The process is to look at these miracles as objectively as possible and be convinced in the depths of our hearts that Jesus did these unbelievable things for people when they asked him. We must be convinced that these miracles were concrete events that actually took place and that the people who received these miracles were ordinary people who trusted Jesus. Once we trust Jesus we can ask him for what we deeply desire. We can put him to the test to see if he will do for us what he did for those in the gospels.

This process makes considerable demands on us, as real trust is painful. This trust requires that we take a risk – the risk that we might be let down. What we need to do is to support our fragile confidence with the examples that Matthew documents. These stories will give us confidence as we read how Jesus rewarded a trusting heart; he did not let down those who trusted him. If we look at the list and honestly believe in them, we will slowly grow in trust and inevitably come to the awareness that Jesus wants to do the same for us also.

We all need proof of affection – words are not enough. By looking at the concrete examples we will see clearly how much Jesus cared for others. Then, by looking again and again, eventually we will become convinced that it is now our turn to step forward and ask Jesus to be as demonstrative towards us in our personal lives as he was to these others.

The depth of conviction is intense and demanding. Because it is so demanding, in practice we cannot request proof from Jesus on an array of issues. There is no limit on Jesus' part, but from ours there are psychological and emotional limits. Therefore, it makes sense to ask Jesus for intervention in only one, two or three areas in our lives. We are offering up our whole being so it is wise to be pragmatic, to be gentle with ourselves and accept that we must work within our own individual limits and not bring to bear any element of force or strain on ourselves. We all have a tendency to swing between two extremes: on the one hand that of over self-reliant rationalism and on the other that of unbridled emotionalism. Neither extreme is very helpful when learning to develop trust. The trust in Jesus that grows from meditating on the things that he did for others is slow to emerge, unspectacular and almost mundane, yet it profoundly affects our whole lives. We should take the first step along this road of trust gently, feeling safe and secure, not bold nor brazen, reminding ourselves constantly that Jesus did miraculous things for others so why not for us? Put that to him and await his response.

The issues that we ask divine help on may seem to be quite simple, even trivial on the surface, but for us they must carry the full weight of our being. We deeply want Jesus to touch this issue for us; we are reaching out to him in great trust so there is nothing trivial about our request. On the other hand, the issues may be complex. Appearances are not important, what matters is our level of investment; how deeply we desire the miracle; our consistency; our patience; and our persistence.

Some requests may take years to be granted, others may be resolved almost immediately. When a miracle is granted, it then goes into our very being as a proof, a certainty, that Jesus truly cares about us. We need these proofs. They address our soul and speak to it about the truth of Jesus' love for us. They fill us with the conviction that we were right to risk trusting Jesus; he has not let us down on this issue so it makes sense to trust him on other issues. Our faith receives a huge boost and our confidence in the existence of the spiritual world is strengthened.

Surely this is a quest worth embarking on. If our trust

is strong we will have our requests granted, our miracle realised, and the promises Jesus made about true happiness fulfilled. Let us rise to the challenge, ask Jesus for a miracle and let our trust in him be tested.

The reward will be ours.

❧ THE PROGRAMME ❧

This is a programme we could follow when we have decic
to ask Jesus to intervene in our lives and give us the grace
of a miracle. The programme has two steps: meditating on
miracles in St Matthew's Gospel, and saying a prayer requesting a miracle, as recommended by Padre Pio.

STEP ONE: MEDITATING ON MIRACLES IN
ST MATTHEW'S GOSPEL

Find a relaxed time during the day, maybe last thing at
night or first thing in the morning, and read a miracle
from the list provided in the last section of this chapter
(see p.26). Allow the story in this miracle to seep deep
into your being. See how the people in that story benefited
from trusting Jesus and believe that you too can have a
miracle given to you if you have the courage to trust Jesus
as they did. Allow yourself to be inspired and believe in
your soul that he will not let you down. Ponder all this,
make it your own, feel energised and resolve to take the
chance to ask Jesus for what you dearly desire. Sometimes
it may be helpful to scan through the whole list and get a
sense of the consistency with which Jesus granted miracles.
You will see how he keeps saying the same thing over and
over again: trust me and I shall not let you down.

STEP TWO: A PRAYER FOR OUR PARTICULAR MIRACLE

When we want to ask for our miracle, a prayer format is very useful; it focuses our thoughts on exactly what it is we are requesting and it allows easy repetition. The prayer in this programme may be recited at any time of day and does not require complete solitude. This prayer will encapsulate the essence of our trust in Jesus. It starts as a mental prayer but soon, through sheer repetition and resolve, becomes a vehicle that allows us to dive into the depths of our innermost selves and stir a conviction that Jesus, the man in the gospel stories who did these supernatural and incomprehensible things, is there for us right now. He is listening and eager to support and encourage our fledgling trust, and will grant us our request. This prayer was used daily by Padre Pio when asking for divine intervention for people in his care. It will foster a total confidence and help us to grow daily in trust. We can recite this prayer once or twice per day, or as often as feels comfortable. The prayer is:

O my Jesus, you have said: 'Truly I say to you, ask and it will be given to you, seek and you will find, knock and it will open to you.' Behold I knock, I seek and ask for the grace of ...
Our Father ... Hail Mary ... Glory be to the Father ... Sacred Heart of Jesus, I place all my trust in you.

O my Jesus, you have said: 'Truly I say to you, if you ask anything of the Father in my name, he will give it to you.' Behold, in your name, I ask the Father for the grace of…

Our Father … Hail Mary … Glory be to the Father … Sacred Heart of Jesus, I place all my trust in you.

O my Jesus, you have said: 'Truly I say to you, heaven and earth will pass away but My words will not pass away.' Encouraged by your infallible words I now ask for the grace of…

Our Father … Hail Mary … Glory be to the Father … Sacred Heart of Jesus, I place all my trust in you.

O Sacred Heart of Jesus, for whom it is impossible not to have compassion on the afflicted, have pity on us and grant us the grace which we ask of you, through the Sorrowful and Immaculate Heart of Mary, your tender Mother and ours.

Say the *Hail, Holy Queen* and add, *St Joseph, foster father of Jesus, pray for us.*

Apart from the times when we are meditating on a miracle in St Matthew's Gospel or saying the prayer, we should have a general attitude of confidence that Jesus has heard our request and will grant it to us. This is a bedrock disposition of trust that allows us to go about our daily business with a degree of peace, despite our daily problems, for we know that Jesus will soon show us in a concrete way that he is there for us. He will grant us the miracle we desire.

TRUST

Trust is fundamental to all the miracles Jesus performed, so it is important to develop a strong sense of what trust actually is. The trust that Jesus wants us to have in him goes beyond what we normally understand trust to be. Trust is not an emotional response nor is it an intellectual response. It draws on both these human elements but demands much more. The trust that we need is something that happens on a deeply intuitive level and encompasses all aspects of our spiritual, mental and emotional worlds. In its purest form, it is better understood as an awareness or fundamental disposition. By its very nature, it is peaceful and deeply empowering. We feel no need to proclaim it from the rooftops or desire that others should recognise it. It is a highly personal experience that is sufficient unto itself. While Jesus always calls us to this highest level of trust, he is also fully aware that we are limited human beings with deeply entrenched habits, fears and needs, and that we can only work within these limits.

TRUST AND MIRACLES

When we have a deeply felt desire to have a miracle granted and we are inspired to persist quietly in our request, then we are motivated by genuine trust and that request will be granted. When our trust is equal to our request, Jesus will invariably respond to us by granting the miracle. He knows this will inspire and encourage us enormously and hence he is eager to make this response.

However, when we overstretch our inner level of trust and try to force a trust that is not authentic, we will feel no inner peace or any level of certitude; instead we will feel anxiety and impatience. Inevitably, Jesus will gently encourage us to move away from such a request. So we have to strike a balance between being true to ourselves and honest to our present position and stirring ourselves to take the risk of moving into the unknown. We have to be willing to explore our own reserves and resolve and, with confidence and honesty, find that spark of trust that is uniquely ours and *then* approach Jesus. By following the suggested programme or some other similar daily practice, we can fan that spark into a fire.

MIRACLES ARE NOT A CURE-ALL

It would be very human to think that having a miracle granted would result in our whole life being transformed and all our problems solved. This would be a very understandable, but nonetheless mistaken, response. When a miracle is granted, that particular area of our life is brought in line with our deepest wishes but all the other facets of our life, although profoundly influenced, go on as before.

We still get up in the morning and face the daily ups and downs that life brings. What changes is our conviction that Jesus really is there, caring intensely about us as individuals, and that he has actually demonstrated his existence to us beyond any doubt. This gives us the courage to go about our everyday lives with a deeper level of peace and confidence than before; now we know for sure that, come what may, we will be safe because Jesus loves us. Miracles aid this growth in faith and it is important to realise that this is their primary function. Although they are outside our normal life experience, that should not mean they are elevated to a status beyond their rightful position. It would be misguided to worship miracles in themselves and somehow see them as an end and not as a means to the end of growing in faith in Jesus.

MIRACLES IN ST MATTHEW'S GOSPEL, WITH COMMENTARIES

JESUS CLEANSES A LEPER MT. 8:1–3

When Jesus had come down from the mountain, great crowds followed him; and there was a leper who came to him and knelt before him, saying, 'Lord, if you choose, you can make me clean.' He stretched out his hand and touched him, saying, 'I do choose. Be made clean!' Immediately his leprosy was cleansed.

✳ COMMENTARY ✳

'I do choose. Be made clean!' – such a human thing to say! Jesus is so friendly to this man, so unselfconscious, unguarded and open. It is the kind of response that someone would give to a brother or sister or close friend; equal to equal. Jesus is always filled with the desire to make life better for us, to help us. He knows that for him to do that, all we have to do is trust him. Isn't it amazing how many times and in how many ways he tells us that, and yet we never seem to hear him? It is such a simple message and yet we cannot take it in; we cannot respond with a totally full-hearted 'Yes!'

JESUS HEALS A CENTURION'S SERVANT
MT. 8:5–13

When he entered Capernaum, a centurion came to him, appealing to him and saying, 'Lord, my servant is lying at home paralysed, in terrible distress.' And he said to him, 'I will come and cure him.' The centurion answered, 'Lord, I am not worthy to have you come under my roof; but only speak the word, and my servant will be healed. For I also am a man under authority, with soldiers under me; and I say to one, "Go", and he goes, and to another, "Come", and he comes, and to my slave, "Do this", and the slave does it.' When Jesus heard him, he was amazed and said to those who followed him, 'Truly I tell you, in no one in Israel have I found such faith …' And to the centurion Jesus said, 'Go; let it be done for you according to your faith.' And the servant was healed in that hour.

❈ COMMENTARY ❈

Jesus was astounded by the centurion's display of utter conviction that he could cure his servant. The centurion knew in his soul that Jesus had the power to order this cure. He simply did not doubt it. He trusted Jesus completely and Jesus responded to that trust. We too must find that level of trust and belief in Jesus and he will assuredly respond to us.

Jesus was astounded because he so rarely met such a

degree of trust. Trust like that is a deeply personal move-ment of the heart. No one, not even Jesus, can cause such unconditional trust: it is the very essence of the individual that reaches out. Jesus appeals and appeals but ultimately it is up to us if we want to respond. Most of the time the re-sponse Jesus gets is guarded and lukewarm. So when some-one like the centurion so wholeheartedly responds, Jesus is taken by surprise. If we want Jesus to intervene in our lives and grant us a miracle then act like the centurion. Let us be big! Let us astonish him with full-blooded trust.

JESUS STILLS THE STORM MT. 8:23–26

And when he got into the boat, his disciples followed him. A gale arose on the lake, so great that the boat was being swamped by the waves; but he was asleep. And they went and woke him up, saying, 'Lord, save us! We are perishing!' And he said to them, 'Why are you afraid, you of little faith?' Then he got up and rebuked the winds and the sea; and there was a dead calm.

❈ COMMENTARY ❈

It was no ordinary storm that broke out; it was an ex-tremely violent one, enough to terrify the most hardened fishermen. Jesus asks his disciples for a level of trust that is very demanding on their inner resources. Even though this demand is extreme, as drowning seemed imminent, Jesus is still harsh on their lack of trust. He does not say, 'I know you are terrified and rightly so in such conditions', instead he says, 'Why are you afraid?' What else would he expect them to feel? However, he really does expect them to feel a sense of security because of his constant caring presence. He is genuinely disappointed, even irritated – 'you of little faith'!

Jesus has very high expectations. If we want him to say to us, 'men of strong faith', we must dig deeper than what we might think is reasonable. That is what he wants. That is the level we must reach in order to impress him.

JESUS HEALS A PARALYTIC MT. 9:2–8

And just then some people were carrying a paralysed man lying on a bed. When Jesus saw their faith, he said to the paralytic, 'Take heart, son; your sins are forgiven … But so that you may know that the Son of Man has authority on earth to forgive sins' – he then said to the paralytic – 'Stand up, take your bed and go to your home.' And he stood up and went to his home. When the crowds saw it, they were filled with awe, and they glorified God, who had given such authority to human beings.

Some men brought Jesus an ill friend and 'when Jesus saw their faith' he cured him. These people had great compassion for their friend and believed that Jesus had the power to perform miracles. They reached out to him; they took the chance that he would not let them down. At this remove, we might easily dismiss the level of risk they took and say, well, of course Jesus would cure the man. However, at the time there would have been many conflicting reports about Jesus and his powers. Nevertheless, these men found the courage and trust to approach him and ask his help for their friend. Their reward was great. Let us follow their example and trust in Jesus.

A GIRL RESTORED TO LIFE AND A WOMAN HEALED MT. 9:18–26

While he was saying these things to them, suddenly a leader of the synagogue came in and knelt before him, saying, 'My daughter has just died; but come and lay your hand on her, and she will live.' And Jesus got up and followed him, with his disciples. Then suddenly a woman who had been suffering from haemorrhages for twelve years came up behind him and touched the fringe of his cloak, for she said to herself, 'If I only touch his cloak, I will be made well.' Jesus turned, and seeing her he said, 'Take heart, daughter; your faith has made you well.' And instantly the woman was made well. When Jesus came to the leader's house and saw the flute-players and the crowd making a commotion, he said, 'Go away; for the girl is not dead but sleeping.' And they laughed at him. But when the crowd had been put outside, he went in and took her by the hand, and the girl got up. And the report of this spread throughout that district.

✳ COMMENTARY ✳

The official displayed great faith in Jesus. His daughter was actually dead; that should have been the end of all hope. But instead, the official believed that all Jesus had to do was lay his hand on her and she would live again. Very, very few people in any age would believe in their hearts that this could happen. Yet this was the level of trust the official had; he believed when hope was almost gone. When the crowd actually laughed at Jesus for saying the girl was sleeping, what must this father have felt? Did he not begin to feel foolish for trusting someone who everyone else seemed to think was some kind of a lunatic? But he did not, he continued on and brought Jesus into his house to where his dead child lay. His reward for trusting Jesus so completely was that his daughter was brought back to life. Can we find the courage to trust even when all hope seems to be gone? This is the challenge.

The woman who was constantly bleeding also went beyond what might be called rational limits. She believed all she had to do was touch Jesus' cloak and she would be cured. She was right.

JESUS HEALS TWO BLIND MEN
MT. 9:27–30

As Jesus went on from there, two blind men followed him, crying loudly, 'Have mercy on us, Son of David!' When he entered the house, the blind men came to him; and Jesus said to them, 'Do you believe that I am able to do this?' They said to him, 'Yes, Lord.' Then he touched their eyes and said, 'According to your faith let it be done to you.' And their eyes were opened.

✺ COMMENTARY ✺

'According to your faith' – again, Jesus links trust in him to the granting of a miracle. He pushes these men to overcome any residual doubt or fear and openly come down on the side of trust. 'Do you believe I am able to do this?' 'Yes, Lord', was their answer. If they had said that they were not sure but they thought they would ask anyway, what would Jesus' response have been?

FEEDING THE FIVE THOUSAND
MT. 14:15–21

When it was evening, the disciples came to him and said, 'This is a deserted place, and the hour is now late; send the crowds away so that they may go into the villages and buy food for themselves.' Jesus said to them, 'They need not go away; you give them something to eat.' They replied, 'We have nothing here but five loaves and two fish.' And he said, 'Bring them here to me.' Then he ordered the crowds to sit down on the grass. Taking the five loaves and the two fish, he looked up to heaven, and blessed and broke the loaves, and gave them to the disciples, and the disciples gave them to the crowds. And all ate and were filled; and they took up what was left over of the broken pieces, twelve baskets full. And those who ate were about five thousand men.

✳ COMMENTARY ✳

Yet again Jesus pushes his disciples to find a deeper faith: 'you give them something to eat'. He knew perfectly well that they could not possibly have anything near the amount necessary to feed well over five thousand people and, to top it all, they were in a lonely place. Yet he suggests that they should feed the crowd. It is almost comical. But what Jesus was doing was focusing the disciples on what is always the solution to their problems: trust in him. Their first reaction had been to suggest a practical solution: 'Send the crowds away'. This did not require any act of trust in him. Jesus was saying that even in the most unlikely occasions turning to him should always be our first response when we are faced with a problem.

JESUS WALKS ON THE WATER
MT. 14:25–31

And early in the morning he came walking towards them on the lake. But when the disciples saw him walking on the lake, they were terrified, saying, 'It is a ghost!' And they cried out in fear. But immediately Jesus spoke to them and said, 'Take heart, it is I; do not be afraid.'

Peter answered him, 'Lord, if it is you, command me to come to you on the water.' He said, 'Come.' So Peter got out of the boat, started walking on the water, and came towards Jesus. But when he noticed the strong wind, he became frightened, and beginning to sink, he cried out, 'Lord, save me!' Jesus immediately reached out his hand and caught him, saying to him, 'You of little faith, why did you doubt?'

※ COMMENTARY ※

When the disciples saw Jesus walking on the lake defying the normal laws of physics, they were terrified. They were terrified because they did not have enough trust in Jesus. If they had, they would not have been surprised at anything they saw him doing. Peter starts out with a determination to trust Jesus but quickly pulls back. Jesus wants total trust in him; he wants no room for doubt. The link between the degree of trust and the granting of a miracle is very clear in this scene. Once Peter entertains doubts, the miracle stops. It is as though the doubt upsets a very delicate balance on which the miracle is poised. For a miracle to be granted trust must be rock solid. Jesus points to this when he chastises Peter: 'You of little faith, why did you doubt?' Jesus is saying that this is the reason Peter began to sink. Peter himself blocked the miracle! So we can learn from this that if we trust Jesus and do not allow doubt to paralyse us then we will receive our miracle. Jesus wants to grant the miracle but sometimes we ourselves stop him. Our doubt breaks the all-important link of trust.

THE CANAANITE WOMAN'S FAITH
MT. 15:21–28

Jesus left that place and went away to the district of Tyre and Sidon. Just then a Canaanite woman from that region came out and started shouting, 'Have mercy on me, Lord, Son of David; my daughter is tormented by a demon.' But he did not answer her at all. And his disciples came and urged him, saying, 'Send her away, for she keeps shouting after us.'

Jesus then decides to test the determination of this woman by treating her in a supposedly off-hand manner:

'I was sent only to the lost sheep of the House of Israel.' But she came and knelt before him, saying, 'Lord, help me.' He answered, 'It is not fair to take the children's food and throw it to the dogs.' She said, 'Yes, Lord, yet even the dogs eat the crumbs that fall from their master's table.' Then Jesus answered her, 'Woman, great is your faith! Let it be done for you as you wish.' And her daughter was healed instantly.

❋ COMMENTARY ❋

This is a powerful example of just how much Jesus wants us to persist to gain the grace we heartily desire. But why does he want such persistence? Why is he not happy with our first, genuine, plea? The surest way to develop that deep inner commitment to trust in Jesus comes through dogged persistence. By sheer repetition, our whole awareness becomes infused with this commitment to trust. We need this level of saturation; it becomes part of our normal thinking process, it forms the basis of our conscious world. With such a mindset, it becomes not a matter of 'if', but 'when', will Jesus grant our request. There is something about the Canaanite woman's manner that tells us she was full of this attitude; she was sure she was going to have her daughter healed. She is almost humorous: there is no sense of panic, she is relaxed and confident and Jesus delights in her unashamed confidence and boldness. Can we be as persistent? Why not!

Jesus Cures a Boy with a Demon Mt. 17:14–20

When they came to the crowd, a man came to him, knelt before him, and said, 'Lord, have mercy on my son, for he is an epileptic and he suffers terribly; he often falls into the fire and often into the water. And I brought him to your disciples, but they could not cure him.' Jesus answered, 'You faithless and perverse generation, how much longer must I be with you? How much longer must I put up with you? Bring him here to me.' And Jesus rebuked the demon, and it came out of him, and the boy was cured instantly.

Then the disciples came to Jesus privately and said, 'Why could we not cast it out?' He said to them, 'Because of your little faith. For truly I tell you, if you have faith the size of a mustard seed, you will say to this mountain, "Move from here to there", and it will move; and nothing will be impossible for you.'

✳ Commentary ✳

This has to be the definitive example of what Jesus is asking of us; the quality of the response he is looking for. He wants a trust that is so much part of our being that we would never consider being denied anything we ask for, literally anything, no matter how bizarre. How insane does it sound to ask a mountain to throw itself into the sea? Yet he tells us it will. We could ask for yesterday to become today or the Statue of Liberty to change places with the Eiffel Tower, and he tells us these things would happen.

In this story, Jesus is angry and frustrated at the lack of wholehearted response. Even his disciples, who have every reason to have unquestioning trust in him, are found wanting. They cannot rise to the level of trust that Jesus wants: they hold back, afraid to believe fully. The message he is trying to get across has not penetrated into their souls; it is still somewhere outside them. They are not embracing Jesus totally and completely. One would be forgiven for excusing them considering they had shown such trust and confidence in him on so many occasions and had endured so much rejection and ridicule. Yet no, Jesus does not spare them: he tells them that their faith is lacking in depth.

This is the problem we all face. Despite our best intentions we cannot fully trust Jesus. We do not experience that inner swell of acceptance of all that Jesus is and offers. That inner 'yes' that allows us to spontaneously trust him beyond the realms of any doubt, is not ours. Such a trust would allow us to ask him for any miracle and he would grant it to us. That degree of trust is our goal: it is the relationship we want to have with Jesus; it is the relationship he wants to have with us. If we start along the road by asking him for our own modest personal miracles, one day we will reach the stage where moving mountains will seem commonplace.

JESUS HEALS TWO BLIND
MEN MT. 20:29–34

As they were leaving Jericho, a large crowd followed. There were two blind men sitting by the roadside. When they heard that Jesus was passing by, they shouted, 'Lord, have mercy on us, Son of David!' The crowd sternly ordered them to be quiet; but they shouted even more loudly, 'Have mercy on us, Lord, Son of David!' Jesus stood still and called them, saying, 'What do you want me to do for you?' They said to him, 'Lord, let our eyes be opened.' Moved with compassion, Jesus touched their eyes. Immediately they regained their sight and followed him.

✳ COMMENTARY ✳

These blind men had to persist, firstly to get past the crowd that wanted them to stay quiet, and then with Jesus himself who made them spell out what they wanted. But why did Jesus want them to articulate their need? What Jesus was looking for was persistence, that determination to stretch themselves and reach out in total trust. These blind men were certainly prepared to go the extra distance and shout out loudly their hearts' desires, so much so that Jesus was moved to feel pity for them. We need that degree of persistence and determination and sheer confidence that he will heed us when we approach him. We should also never underestimate the humanity of Jesus when we ask him for a miracle. We must lay out our plight in all its stark pain and confusion. If our hearts are true, sometimes he may simply be moved by compassion to grant our request.

JESUS CURSES THE FIG TREE MT. 21:18–22

In the morning, when he returned to the city, he was hungry. And seeing a fig tree by the side of the road, he went to it and found nothing at all on it but leaves. Then he said to it, 'May no fruit ever come from you again!' And the fig tree withered at once. When the disciples saw it, they were amazed, saying, 'How did the fig tree wither at once?' Jesus answered them, 'Truly I tell you, if you have faith and do not doubt, not only will you do what has been done to the fig tree, but even if you say to this mountain, "Be lifted up and thrown into the sea", it will be done. Whatever you ask for in prayer with faith, you will receive.'

※ COMMENTARY ※

Jesus performs what seems to be a very odd miracle: there are no hungry masses that need to be fed; there are no sick people who need to be cured; indeed, there is no need at all to perform this miracle. On top of all that, he does something that seems gratuitous and destructive: he kills a tree!

When the disciples ask him about the poor fig tree, he ignores their sentiments and goes straight to what he wants them to learn: faith underlies all miracles. If we trust him, then all power will be granted to us, to be used even over things that are essentially trivial. Jesus uses this spectacular deed to show this truth. An important clause in what Jesus said was, 'and do not doubt'. He is emphasising the need to have total conviction; a conviction that brings us into such close communion with him that doubt just cannot co-exist with. In this state, literally everything is possible. That is his message.

∞ 2 ∞

MATERIALISM

We eat nothing in the houses of the rich so as to be able to tell the poor when they offer us a drink: 'We do not take anything outside.'

Mother Teresa

❧ INTRODUCTION ❧

The desire for shelter, food and a certain level of security for the future, is a healthy and necessary aspiration for every human being. Materialism, on the other hand, is the excessive accumulation of possessions beyond what may be reasonably considered necessary for living. Jesus advises us against materialism as it inevitably captures our hearts and spiritual realities become shut out.

This is not because there is something intrinsically wrong with material possessions, as was so often the interpretation in the past, but because unbridled materialism so captivates our hearts and minds, that it inevitably leaves little room for spiritual development. Jesus told those he met not to worry about tomorrow but to live a life of freedom of spirit and all other needs would be met by his father.

MATERIALISM

The accumulation and possession of wealth allows us to escape from ourselves. We no longer have to face the difficulties of life if we can insulate ourselves through possessions. As our wealth increases, the range of options to distract ourselves also dramatically increases. We may say that we become addicted to wealth because it provides us with a way to anaesthetise ourselves against our problems.

But, as with any addiction, dependence follows, and with that dependence comes the loss of freedom. The whole focus of our lives can shift onto maintaining and increasing our wealth: we want our possessions; we have grown to need them; we cannot imagine a life without them; we are frightened of losing them. Jesus advises us not to give our hearts to material possessions, not to subordinate our spirits to the material world. He wants us to value freedom of spirit over transitory comforts, even if it means having to be tougher on ourselves on the material level.

As we accumulate possessions, they become more and more part of our identity. We become more aware of our standing with others and how our wealth compares to theirs. Increases in wealth, even modest ones, bring with them increases in status. Naturally, we do not want to lose our special status; we become comfortable in our position in society and want to maintain it. But Jesus tells us that if we want this, it comes at a price. If we want to be treated as special, if we want high status, we will inevitably give our hearts to achieve that end. But when we give our hearts to the accumulation of material possessions, we lose a certain sensitivity towards the needs of those less well off. As we become more preoccupied with our own drive towards more, we care less about those around us. When we do give of our wealth but still remain highly wealthy, there is a contradiction between our giving and our indulgence. We may even take on the battle for the poor, but if we ourselves remain indulgent in possessions, the contradiction becomes even more acute. We become caught in a very subtle web of self-deception. We see our wealth and conclude that we have a responsibility to assist others. As we gain further notoriety for our charitable deeds and our status increases, we are inclined to focus even more intently on ourselves. We become so preoccupied with status and wealth that we are truly blinded to spiritual realities.

With the accumulation of wealth, we tend to come to an inner belief that we can have absolute security: that we can secure our lives and our futures and protect ourselves and our loved ones in life. As we centre our psychological and emotional life more and more on material possessions, we develop a sense that wealth can bring us this desired security. Thus, we start to transfer our trust away from any spiritual dimension and place it solidly in the material. We believe our future will be secured despite the everyday reality that life continues to throw up the unexpected.

To achieve lasting security we need to place our trust in something or someone that can deliver it; clearly, materialism cannot. The deep sense of security that we all desire is an internal disposition; it is a feeling that all is well despite what may be going on in our everyday lives. It is awareness that somehow there is a reason to all we experience, that our lives are not random, that we count and that we have an intrinsic worth beyond all relative circumstances. It is an experience beyond the here-and-now, which is not dependent on the events of our lives running smoothly. No amount of control over our present or future destinies can give us this experience of deep inner security.

Jesus calls us to trust him for he alone is trustworthy. Everything else we turn to will inevitably let us down. As christians, we can be comfortable with the relative insecurities of life if we place our trust in Jesus, who promises to be our rock.

LIVING A NON-MATERIALISTIC LIFE

If we want to know where we stand with regard to materialism, whether we have a balanced approach or whether we are tending toward excess, then we should ask ourselves this simple question: Where do our hearts lie? To answer this question honestly we need to take time to reflect on our lives and our motivations. We need to understand what drives us, what we want in life, what our priorities are. We may not be excessively wealthy but our hearts may still be captivated by our possessions. What is important is that we acknowledge the truth of our position with regard to materialism. If we feel we are living a life too centred on materialism then we need to examine what we can do to address the imbalance. The simple programme that follows later in this chapter is a suggested way to do this. It is based on materialism in St Mark's and St Luke's gospels.

Fundamentally, we are not looking for mechanical adjustments in our behaviour; that is, we are not trying to change the way we live our lives. What we desire to bring about is a change in the spirit in which we live them. We are seeking to re-orientate our hearts so that we believe, with total conviction, that a less materialistic life is fuller and freer and will allow us to experience the peace and security that Jesus promised. However, any form of change that is motivated by purely intellectual conviction will inevitably be dry and impoverished and will have little spiritual value. This is always a danger, despite the best of intentions. The change of heart that we desire is, by its very nature, subtle and even elusive. In a real sense, non-materialism has to find us, as opposed to us finding it. We cannot force it; we can only ponder Jesus' words and let them seep into our hearts. We can then honestly put before him our disposition towards materialism and ask him to awaken our spiritual awareness.

When we are moved to set limits to our material wants and desires, and to pass on any excess wealth to those who are in need, we begin to unburden ourselves of all the associated difficulties of wealth. When we can say that as long as we have adequate shelter, nourishment and reasonable provisions for the future for ourselves and for those in our care we will be content, then we will start to experience peace. When we truly desire limits to our wants, not confusing them with our needs, we will experience a freedom, a sense of being part of humanity, equal to all and superior to none. Every day will be as before, full of the normal cares of life; but we will meet it with no fear, with no desire to build an ever-increasing wall of protection. We will face life with courage and optimism, alive and vital with lightness and cheerfulness.

A strong method for stirring our hearts to redress our attitude towards materialism is to look at our lives with a sense of gratitude as we ponder the many graces we enjoy (in the following programme is a prayer of gratitude that might help us do this). We should take some time to consider the warmth and love we are fortunate to have from our family and friends and how their love gives meaning to our lives. We should ask ourselves what our lives would be like without such love. In the normal course of our daily lives, how often are our psychological batteries recharged by the warmth of innumerable human exchanges? We should reflect, if we are fortunate enough, on the fact that we have the following: shelter to protect us from the elements; a bed to sleep in; adequate food to eat; sufficient good health to allow us go out and breathe fresh air; an intellect that can help us appreciate literature, music, science, our culture, the cultures of other peoples, good from bad, and right from wrong. Feeling a deep sense of gratitude for all we have may inspire us to thank Jesus. We may stop for a while and give our hearts to him as an expression of this gratitude; withdraw our mental energies from thoughts of progress in the future or schemes to improve our lives; live in the present reality of the gifts he has given us. Simply saying a heartfelt thank you for what we have will help us to focus on non-materialism.

How literal should our interpretation of Jesus' advice be? This is a question that we will inevitably ask ourselves once we decide to embrace a non-materialistic life. There is no simple answer to this question as it depends entirely on what our honest response is to the movement of our hearts. If we feel no desire to move away from the pursuit of possessions, then it is better to be an honest materialist than a deluded non-materialist.

Essentially, non-materialism is a grace, which we can desire but cannot demand. For example, Mother Teresa was filled with a desire to live life in close proximity to the poorest of the poor. On the question of health insurance for her sisters, Mother Teresa replied, 'No, that is not for us … Do the poor that we work with have health insurance?' For most of us such a life would be too extreme; we could not honestly live it. We do need to challenge ourselves but yet respect our own circumstances and mental dispositions. We need to allow ourselves to be inspired by people like Mother Teresa and yet retain a sense of responsibility towards our own practical lives. We need to push ourselves and yet be gentle with ourselves. Our aim is not to deny

ourselves material comforts, but to embrace spiritual freedom.

When we look into the eyes of children and see the
sheer joy of life they are experiencing we should realise
that this is what Jesus wants for us too. We must strive to
become like them and see only the adventure that life is.
We must learn again to live for today and not worry excessively about where our food, shelter or security will come
from. Jesus desires this for us so much, and has told us
insistently that he loves us and wants to take care of us. We
can open our hearts and embrace life, shed our fears and
allow happiness to engulf us, secure in the knowledge that
Jesus knows our needs and will always protect us.

This is a suggested programme that may help us nurture a non-materialistic life. The programme has two steps: meditating on materialism in St Mark's and St Luke's gospels; and saying a simple prayer of gratitude before meals.

STEP ONE: MEDITATING ON MATERIALISM IN ST MARK'S AND ST LUKE'S GOSPELS

When you feel inspired to consider in practical terms the direction of your life with regard to materialism, read one of the gospel extracts at the end of this chapter (see p. 56). Allow Jesus' words to descend deep into your mind. As you dwell on what Jesus is saying let your awareness go to your heart and feel any movement that takes place there. Be aware that only when our hearts are won over can any meaningful action follow. So be gentle with yourself, relax and trust that the changes you desire will take place. Jesus wants our hearts; he wants us to experience the freedom of spirit that he has promised. All we have to do is open the door and let our hearts be stirred by him.

STEP TWO: A PRAYER BEFORE MEALS

This simple prayer, in one of its various forms, was learned by children in the past. It was said before every meal as an acknowledgement of, and gratitude for, the gift of the food that was about to be eaten. Perhaps for many of us today it has dropped out of use. But saying this prayer in the quietness of our hearts can help us develop an attitude of warm gratitude to Jesus. This gratitude can also permeate through our day when we stir our hearts to follow Jesus along the road of non-materialism. The prayer is:

We give you thanks Almighty God for these your gifts that we are about to receive, through Christ Our Lord. Amen.

Or simply:

Thank you, Lord.

∽ NOTES ∾

THE MISTAKE OF PAST INTERPRETATION

With the passage of time, the interpretation of what Jesus had to say about a non-materialistic life became focused on the simple denial of possessions, but neglected to give the reasons for this. This led to the perception that the non-materialistic life was essentially a joyless negation of the pleasures of life. What was not generally understood was that the real purpose of such a life was to liberate the spirit so that a profound freedom could be experienced. Because of this general lack of understanding, the form of a non-materialistic life was lived but the spirit was absent. This indeed led to a joyless life with all hope of happiness being postponed until the next life.

Today, this view still has a powerfully negative influence, making the understanding of non-materialism much more difficult. We are inclined to think that previous generations lived by this diktat and were unhappy and unfulfilled as a result, leading us to think that we should enjoy the pleasures of life and embrace material prosperity with open arms. What we need to do is look closely again at what Jesus had to say about materialism. See how he always emphasised the spiritual life when he talked about materialism and did not just reject the acquisition of possessions. See the compassion he had for those caught in the grip of materialism. See how his concern was always for people's spiritual welfare.

Today, Jesus wants us to live life to the full, here and now. He does not want us simply to endure life by making it hard for ourselves. He wants us to experience the essence of life, which is the spiritual dimension with no diminishing of that experience due to any dullness of heart.

MATERIALISM IN ST MARK'S AND ST LUKE'S GOSPELS, WITH COMMENTARIES

THE RICH MAN MK. 10:17–22

As Jesus was setting out on a journey, a man ran up and knelt before him, and asked, 'Good Teacher, what must I do to inherit eternal life?' Jesus said to him, 'Why do you call me good? No one is good but God alone. You know the commandments: "You shall not murder; You shall not commit adultery; You shall not steal; You shall not bear false witness; You shall not defraud; Honour your father and mother".' He said to him, 'Teacher, I have kept all these since my youth.' Jesus, looking at him, loved him and said, 'You lack one thing; go, sell what you own, and give the money to the poor, and you will have treasure in heaven; then come, follow me.' When he heard this, he was shocked and went away grieving, for he had many possessions.

※ COMMENTARY ※

We can learn almost all that Jesus had to teach about materialism from this extract from St Mark's Gospel. Put simply: materialism makes a captive of our hearts.

This man was obviously very enthusiastic about Jesus.

He ran up to him, kneeled before him, and acknowledged him as a spiritual master. He may even have believed that Jesus was the Messiah. He appears to have been a person who had already made a decision that he was prepared to make far-reaching changes in his life to progress spiritually. He was a good man but he was in a hurry; he wanted action, he wanted Jesus to talk straight and give him clear direction. In a very public way he knelt before Jesus, opened his heart and told him how he had lived his life to date. But perhaps he was a little impatient and was looking for a ready-made solution to spiritual progress. St Luke tells us that he was from a leading family and perhaps he was used to instant gratification without having to make any real effort or with little cost to himself. Jesus tries to slow him down and to get him to reflect on who he was talking to and the enormity of what he was asking for: he was talking to the Messiah who could lead him on a direct road to spiritual awakening.

Jesus felt great love for this man but great pity for him also. He knew how possessions had a hold over this man's heart and no matter how strong his desire for the spiritual life was, he could never break their grip. We might imagine that knowing this, Jesus would have made it a little easier for this rich man by telling him to sell half his possessions. That would have cost him dearly yet left him with sufficient wealth to live in something like the comfort to which he was accustomed. But no, Jesus set the bar at its highest – sell all – and the man left saddened.

But this rich man should have known that Jesus would challenge him. He was clearly intent on following the spiritual path and he was a Jew. From earliest times the Jews had awaited the Messiah. This man knew his faith and would therefore have been predisposed to believe it possible that Jesus was the Messiah, or at the very least, a high calibre prophet. Suspecting then who Jesus was, it is difficult to believe he turned away when Jesus told him he could come with him only after he had sold his possessions. How could such an informed and spiritually motivated man knowingly reject such an invitation? In real and practical terms he walked away from a whole new life; an adventure that promised to be full of vitality and newness in the company of someone he knew to be a great guide. He rejected all this promise and returned to a world that held him captive; 'he was shocked' at Jesus' words and he returned to his riches.

We may think we would have acted differently to this unfortunate rich man but would we? We may think we would not have hesitated for a moment if we were to encounter Jesus physically today and he made us such an offer; but maybe materialism has a stronger hold over us than we are prepared to acknowledge. This rich man probably lived for another fifty years at most and we can only speculate as to how he felt on his deathbed. Did he regret not having delved into the depths of his heart and taken up Jesus' offer? Let us learn from this unfortunate man's experience and resolve to do everything in our power to free our hearts from the grip of materialism.

THE RICH MAN MK. 10:23–27

Then Jesus looked around and said to his disciples, 'How hard it will be for those who have wealth to enter the kingdom of God!' And the disciples were perplexed at these words. But Jesus said to them again, 'Children, how hard it is to enter the kingdom of God! It is easier for a camel to go through the eye of a needle than for someone who is rich to enter the kingdom of God.' They were greatly astounded and said to one another, 'Then who can be saved?' Jesus looked at them and said, 'For mortals it is impossible, but not for God; for God all things are possible.'

✸ COMMENTARY ✸

When Jesus first says how hard it is for a rich man to enter the kingdom of heaven, the disciples are not happy. However, instead of making things a little bit more palatable, he responds by insisting on this. We can conclude then that for Jesus, materialism is a major obstacle on the path of spiritual growth. This should be of great concern to us if we are serious about wanting to follow him and experience spiritual freedom. But because our society takes materialism so much for granted, it is very difficult for us to do the opposite. We are inclined not to want to address this issue at all and, as the rich man in the previous extract, tell ourselves that we do our best. But Jesus would not accept this from the rich man so presumably he would not accept it from us either. He wants more. He wants our hearts. Are we prepared to give them to him?

THE WIDOW'S OFFERING MK. 12:41–44

He sat down opposite the treasury and watched the crowd putting money into the treasury. Many rich people put in large sums. A poor widow came and put in two small copper coins, which are worth a penny. Then he called his disciples and said to them, 'Truly I tell you, this poor widow has put more in than all those who are contributing to the treasury. For all of them have contributed out of their abundance; but she out of her poverty has put in everything she had, all she had to live on.'

※ COMMENTARY ※

In this extract, we see that many rich people gave considerable sums to the treasury. This seems generous and could be taken as an indication of their relative detachment from their wealth. But Jesus, it would appear, was not particularly impressed. They gave from their excess, which put no burden on them personally and demanded no sacrifices. Their actions told him nothing about the movement of their hearts. The actions of the widow, however, told Jesus exactly about the spiritual quality of her heart. She had no attachment to materialism; her heart urged her and she responded by giving all. She knew she had to go home and somehow get by with nothing. But this did not stop her acting in a spirit of generosity.

Jesus has told us that God sees everything we do in private. In the case of this widow, how dramatically true this was for her. God was actually sitting behind her watching! She could never have dreamt that her simple generosity would so profoundly touch Jesus. What would she have felt if she had known that if she turned around she would have looked into the eyes of the Messiah who was watching her with infinite love? What a reward for living life with a free and generous heart! We should be inspired by her and strive to act with such generosity and trust in Jesus for the future. We should give not from our excess but from our poverty. We should push ourselves and give until it hurts and believe that Jesus, just as he was with the widow, is sitting there looking on approvingly.

THE PARABLE OF THE RICH FOOL
LK. 12:13–21

Someone in the crowd said to him, 'Teacher, tell my brother to divide the family inheritance with me.' But he said to him, 'Friend, who set me to be a judge or arbitrator over you?' And he said to them, 'Take care! Be on your guard against all kinds of greed; for one's life does not consist in the abundance of possessions.' Then he told them a parable: 'The land of a rich man produced abundantly. And he thought to himself, "What should I do, for I have no place to store my crops?" Then he said, "I will do this: I will pull down my barns and build larger ones, and there I will store all my grain and my goods. And I will say to my soul, Soul, you have ample goods laid up for many years; relax, eat, drink, be merry." But God said to him, "You fool! This very night your life is being demanded of you. And the things you have prepared, whose will they be?" So it is with those who store up treasures for themselves but are not rich towards God.'

※ COMMENTARY ※

Materialism leads us to believe that we can secure ourselves against every eventuality. As we accumulate possessions, we see how more and more our lives become insulated from the harsh realities of life. Gradually we grow to feel that security is an attainable goal; that if we have enough resources we can build an impenetrable wall behind which we will be untouchable. Jesus warns us not to be so blinkered. There can be no lasting security in the material world in which everything, by its very nature, is changing.

The parable tells how the rich man decided he would put his feet up and enjoy the fruits of his labour. We might think that maybe that was not such a bad idea. He had obviously worked hard and had been materially successful as a result, so why not plan ahead to indulge a bit? But life does not always allow for such planning and this rich man had no notion of that. He thought it his right to enjoy the fruits of his labour. He was too self-congratulatory; he was happy to believe that he, and he alone, was the author of his own good fortune. He had no sense of gratitude to God or fate or any outside agency. He was obviously a hard-nosed businessman who knew how to get his way and probably felt that those who worked in the fields for him were there only as aids to assist him to fulfil his ambitions. If he had felt any gratitude towards others, he would have realised that it was not because he was totally in control of things that he had accumulated so much. By extension, he would have seen that he was not in control of his future either. He didn't look around at those who had few material possessions and realise that, but for his good fortune, it could have been him.

Nor did he reflect that, had he not been born into the family he was born into and had the education he had, he would not have been able to accumulate such possessions. If he had not been so self-absorbed, he would have reflected on the deaths of people he had known and seen that that too was his ultimate fate. But he was blinded by materialism and only saw a life stretching out into the future with no end. He had given his heart to material possessions and fallen under their intoxicating spell. He had transferred his trust from the spiritual domain and placed it firmly in the material.

DO NOT WORRY LK. 12:22–32

He said to his disciples, 'Therefore I tell you, do not worry about your life, what you will eat, or about your body, what you will wear. For life is more than food, and the body more than clothing. Consider the ravens: they neither sow nor reap, they have neither storehouse nor barn, and yet God feeds them. Of how much more value are you than the birds! And can any of you, by worrying, add a single hour to your span of life? If then, you are not able to do so small a thing as that, why do you worry about the rest? Consider the lilies, how they grow: they neither toil nor spin yet I tell you, even Solomon in all his glory was not clothed like one of these. But if God so clothes the grass of the field, which is alive today and tomorrow is thrown into the oven, how much more will he clothe you – you of little faith! And do not keep striving for what you are to eat and what you are to drink, and do not keep worrying.

'For it is the nations of the world that strive after all these things, and your Father knows that you need them. Instead, strive for his kingdom, and these things will be given to you as well. Do not be afraid, little flock, for it is your Father's good pleasure to give you the kingdom.'

❊ Commentary ❊

This passage encapsulates the spirit of non-materialism. Jesus is extremely relaxed and full of spirit. He appeals to the apostles, in the most poetic language, not to worry about material things. He tells them to put their trust in him and not in materialism. We can feel the freedom of the birds as they fly around with absolutely no consciousness of their vulnerability. We see the flowers attaining splendour with no effort on their part. Jesus is talking from his heart and appealing to the hearts of his apostles. He wants to inspire them and lift them out of the heaviness of heart that the concern for material security brings. He wants them to see clearly that they are being looked after and are not alone, that they should not worry. When he calls them 'men of little faith', we feel that he is only gently jibing them. Usually when he calls them this he means to unsettle them and push them out of their mediocrity. But this time he is full of warmth and eagerness.

We get a real sense of how Jesus feels in his heart; a heart uncluttered and totally free of materialism. Jesus tells us that we need have no concern for our present or our future. We can live a life free from worries about our wealth, our status, our health or our happiness. We can get up in the morning and greet the new day with a heart that is open and at peace. Our hearts will be willing and eager to embrace whatever the day brings for we know and have accepted in the depths of our hearts that we do not control our lives. We have understood, and it has become part of our awareness that we are travellers on a journey through this world and one day we will depart for a different world. We know that all material possessions will cease to have any part of our lives once we die and thus we have not allowed them define us. Jesus tells us not to be afraid, to give our hearts to him and not allow anything to cloud our trust. Of course, we need the basic necessities in life, but what Jesus is warning us against is the excessive accumulation of, and dependence on, possessions.

Jesus loves us with a heart that is soft and gentle. He wants us to come to him with openness and simplicity. He calls us his 'little flock'; we are his children and he wants to look after us. Let us set aside our pretensions, our ambitions, our grandiose image of ourselves and go to him. Let us allow him to put his arms around us, hug him back and walk together to wherever he wants to go.

DO NOT WORRY LK. 12:33–34

'Sell your possessions, and give alms. Make purses for yourselves that do not wear out, an unfailing treasure in heaven, where no thief comes near and no moth destroys. For where your treasure is, there your heart will be also.'

※ COMMENTARY ※

Jesus gives the reason that we should choose a non-materialistic life: 'for where your treasure is, there your heart will be also'. It is for this reason and this reason only that we should curtail our appetites for possessions, for prestige, for status. If we really open our hearts to Jesus' words; if we allow the full meaning of what he is saying to impact on our innermost selves we will find over time an expansive awareness developing in us naturally and spontaneously. We will feel, with no sense of frustration or denial, that we do not want the encumbrance of excessive wealth and status. We will favour the lightness and happiness of a spirit that is free and accepting, a spirit that is content with having normal daily material needs met, with no excessive anxiety for tomorrow.

∞ 3 ∞

FORGIVENESS

When we examine the relationship between mind, or consciousness, and body, we see that the wholesome attitudes, emotions, and states of mind, like compassion, tolerance and forgiveness, are strongly connected with physical health and well-being. They enhance physical well-being, whereas negative or unwholesome attitudes and emotions – anger, hatred, disturbed states of mind – undermine physical health.

The Dalai Lama

❧ INTRODUCTION ❧

We have all been offended in our lives and felt hurt as a result. If the sense of hurt was deeply felt, it can persist for years. This happens when we continually relive the experience of the offence and never allow our psychological and emotional scars to heal; instead, they remain raw and tender. If we allow our thoughts of the offence and of the offender to fester, we will inevitably foster a strong desire to exact revenge. If we take revenge, we risk the offender in his turn offending us again to dissipate his feelings of hurt.

Jesus advised his apostles to forgive those who offended them, thus avoiding this vicious circle. If we want to take Jesus' advice, we need to learn the art of practising forgiveness. Forgiveness is a process and not a single event; it is only by repetition that we eventually make forgiveness our automatic response to any offence.

Understanding offence
and forgiveness

We all carry wounds from offences we suffered in the past. None of us goes through life without encounters with others that have hurt us, sometimes superficially, sometimes deeply. But although the nature of the offences against us may be varied, the hurt we experience is usually the same. We feel let down: our goodwill taken for granted and our trust betrayed. The most deeply felt offences are often those that result from a relationship where trust had grown up and we felt a level of intimacy. In such cases, the hurt can be intense and persistent. Deep hurt pierces through to the very core of our hearts. It lodges there and becomes part of our consciousness. It surfaces – sometimes occasionally, sometimes often. Its influence on us may at times be slight but it is never altogether absent. Jesus tells us that we are all one in him and should love one another and forgive those who offend us. When we are offended, a wedge lodges between us and the offender and unity is broken. Through forgiveness, we allow oneness to be re-established and peace to be restored in our hearts.

Often it is necessary to have this same attitude of forgiveness towards ourselves as self-criticism can also disrupt our inner peace.

It is important to realise that Jesus, in advising forgiveness, is not recommending that we suspend our critical faculties. If we want to follow Jesus' advice and not allow hurt to gain a foothold in our hearts, we should first give ourselves time to reflect on, and come to an understanding of, the nature of the offence against us and the forces that propelled the offender to act as he did. Very often, in a somewhat misguided desire to follow Jesus' words, our first instinct is to forgive immediately and unquestioningly. We feel a certain moral imperative to rush to forgive. This may seem laudable but when it is accompanied by a desire to deny the offence in the first place, it is counter-productive. We may feel it is wrong to reflect on the offence and that it is more morally correct simply to get on with life. But if we do not have a healthy respect for ourselves and fully recognise and acknowledge the hurt, we cannot truly forgive.

The course we choose is characterised by restraint, compassion and empathy towards the offender. Jesus fully comprehended the motivations of his offenders and the nature of the offences against him. It was from this position of wisdom that he forgave them.

When we forgive someone, we are essentially brushing aside their offence and not letting our hearts be captured by feelings of self-pity or hurt, whether justified or unjustified. We are mustering our inner resources to stop ourselves reacting negatively. Our natural tendency to absorb offences and feel hurt gives way to a new inner disposition that encourages us to see the bigger picture and not allow ourselves be tied into the here-and-now of agitated emotions. We are deciding to use our intellect and not just be at the mercy of our inflamed passions. We are deciding to have some understanding of an offender's disposition and motivation to gain an insight into their offending behaviour. We are essentially looking for good, solid reasons not to be insulted but to feel empathy and compassion for the offender.

When we understand why and how a person offended us, we can begin to see things from a broader perspective. We no longer need to remain locked in our own narrow vision of events. We can begin to say that if we had their mental or emotional disposition we too may have acted the way they did. We start identifying with their insensitivity. Jesus certainly did this with those who accused him of untruths and designed to kill him. His response was one of supreme pity and compassion, for he so clearly saw their deep spiritual ignorance.

When Jesus tells us to turn the other cheek when we are offended, in effect what he is saying is: do not offer resistance, do not fight fire with fire, do not offend. If we allow ourselves to be deeply hurt, it will inevitably lead us to feeling anger towards the person who caused it. This anger can then give rise to the desire for revenge. If we give in to the urge to take retaliatory action then instead of the balance that we desired being redressed and scales being brought to a state of equilibrium, we are often plunged into a state of deeper anxiety. Although initially we may feel a sense of gratification that we have repaid like with like, soon that sense will evaporate as we realise that the peace and release from the initial hurt we expected to experience has not materialised. Instead, we feel more tied than ever into the whole, painful affair. For this reason, Jesus tells us not to meet offence head-on but to let it wash over us. By not accepting offences, they become spent forces.

PRACTISING FORGIVENESS TODAY

For most of us, our natural response to an offence is to bristle and feel upset. If instead we want forgiveness to be our first response, then we need to commit ourselves to the practice of forgiveness. Through repeatedly checking our natural tendencies, we allow a deeper, more compassionate response to surface from our hearts. We cannot expect an instant cessation of all negative feelings – which will inevitably continue to arise – but by making the fundamental change in our attitude from one of anger to forgiveness, in time we will see changes in our emotional responses.

Our reaction to an offence may arise strongly and unexpectedly within us, with lightning negativity towards the offender. In reality, we have little chance of heading off such reactions and can only, as soon as we become conscious of our excited state, begin to apply our minds and employ forgiveness. When our disposition towards offence is highly sensitive we will find such unexpected, highly charged reactions dominating us. What we need to do is to build up, through practice, an inner strength that will help us not to accept offence in the first place, thus making the need for forgiveness almost redundant.

The hurt from past offences may manifest itself as negative thoughts within our minds or even register as a physical experience within our bodies. Very often when we find such experiences of discomfort or unrest rising within us we tend to focus on them as though they were a new experience. Our minds have a tendency to treat the thoughts of the past offence and the offender as having just taken place and therefore in need of our full attention.

This cycle of mulling over the experience of hurt repeatedly, keeps the offence fresh and the hurt raw and sensitive. What we need to do is say to ourselves that we have acknowledged and come to an understanding of this offence and have made a decision to forgive it. Essentially, we are doing what Jesus did and advised us to do. We are engaging our minds in the practice of forgiveness, understanding that it is through this practice that we will eventually be freed from the grip of these painful experiences.

In the following section, a programme that may help us to practise forgiveness will be set out. This programme is based on extracts from St Luke's Gospel in which Jesus discusses forgiveness. Jesus told his disciples to make forgiveness their bedrock response to all offences. He advised them to forgive and forgive and forgive, and to continue this practice without ceasing, as he had done. To help us make forgiveness our primary response we should practise seeing the good in those who offend us. Goodness is always there; maybe not directed towards us but perhaps towards others. We may have seen a person who offended us act with empathy towards others. We may know that they work hard to support a family or to achieve goals that benefit others. We should also be aware that their good traits might be directed towards people or things that we know nothing about. What we need to have is a sense of the dignity of the individual even though they may have offended us. We should never assume we know all there is to know or have a dismissive attitude towards those who offend us.

If we believe in the essential goodness of humanity, we will begin to see a degree of this goodness in those who hurt us, and this will encourage us to soften towards them. This will help to redress the emotional imbalance and ease the sting of the hurt that they may have caused us. Ultimately, no war lasts forever; foes of yesterday are friends of today. We can suffer no offence so great that a degree of forgiveness cannot be achieved. Jesus overlooks our shortcomings on a daily basis and he asks us to do the same with those who are insensitive towards us.

If we practise forgiveness we will find that time will change our experience of hurt. If the offence was not too serious then almost certainly time will heal any hurt that may have been caused. If the offence was deeply felt then over time, and with a commitment to forgiveness, our hearts will soften and the hurt that once consumed us will have lost its hold.

Ultimately, for forgiveness to be true we must have forgetfulness. Forgetfulness though cannot be practised for it is not an end in itself but the by-product of true forgiveness. We can and should desire it but we cannot pursue it. Hurt can consume us and cause our spirits continual unrest, making forgetfulness very difficult. We do not expect of ourselves a forgetfulness of a bodily ailment like a toothache so is it unreasonable to expect forgetfulness of a spiritual ailment? To forget deep hurts would be unrealistic for most of us but by encouraging ourselves to forget lesser offences we can increase our tolerance. Ultimately, forgetfulness comes to us when we have softened towards the person who offended us and feel free from the hurt they caused us. We make a distinction between the person and their unacceptable behaviour. Forgetfulness brings peace of spirit; it cleanses our minds and emotions of any residual negative feelings and allows us to restore broken relationships. When forgetfulness is ours, we do not harbour any resentment or bad feelings towards someone who offended us, for we have simply forgotten the offence.

⁂ THE PROGRAMME ⁂

This is a suggested programme that we might follow to help make forgiveness our primary response to any offence. The programme has two steps: meditating on forgiveness in St Luke's Gospel; and saying a prayer about forgiveness. The steps may be used in conjunction with one another or separately.

STEP ONE: MEDITATING ON FORGIVENESS IN ST LUKE'S GOSPEL

Before we take this first step we should call to mind whom it is we wish to forgive and then ask ourselves three simple questions:

1. What was the offence that caused us hurt? (If there were a few, over a long period, just select one main one.)
2. What do we believe motivated the person? (e.g. was it insensitivity, resentment, fear, etc?)
3. Do we truly wish to forgive them?

The reason that we focus on these issues is not to stir up past hurts and relive the negative experience but to have an awareness of what we are undertaking. We want to avoid an over-generalised, hazy attitude towards the person who offended us. For question one, we should not explicitly engage our emotions but should make this a purely intellectual exercise. The reason for this is to prevent old feelings of hurt from re-surfacing. To this end, we should spend as short a time as possible on this part of the exercise. In questions two and three, we should rouse our emotions to encourage feelings of compassion.

Once we have stimulated our minds and stirred our hearts and are genuinely moved to embrace forgiveness towards this person, we should then read one or two extracts on forgiveness (see p.83) and meditate for a short time on them. We should observe how Jesus behaved and let his example seep into our beings. We must then resolve, with all our power, to do as he did and forgive the person in question.

STEP TWO: A PRAYER ABOUT FORGIVENESS

Once we have meditated on forgiveness, it is then helpful to let our hearts reach out to Jesus in prayer.

Sometimes we find ourselves in the grip of the emotion of hurt; we are consumed by feelings of injury, broken trust, anger or even revenge. At such times, we should turn to Jesus as best we can in prayer. We should tell him we do not want to feel this way and ask him to be merciful towards us and free us from these disturbing emotions. Our tone should express the depth of our faith in him. He will help us to forgive and move on from this painful experience. A suitable prayer is:

Jesus, help me to forgive.

Or simply,

Jesus Christ.

In times of greater recollection, when we feel less troubled, we can develop an attitude of forgiveness by repeating several times and letting sink into our being the lines from the Our Father on forgiveness:

Forgive us our trespasses as we forgive those who trespass against us.

TYPES OF OFFENCE

People may offend us for a variety of reasons. One possibility is that they might be ignorant of our sensibilities: they simply do not realise how offended we can be by their words or deeds. Also people may offend us because of their identification with an ideology or a certain way of life or behaviour that we do not share; because of their beliefs, they may be intolerant of us and offend us. Another possibility is that people can be so absorbed in themselves that they are virtually incapable of ever putting other people's interests before their own.

Sometimes no offence is actually intended. We all have a sensitivity to offences that are the result of our past emotional experiences. This sensitivity can make it difficult for us to know if someone actually offended us or, because of our own disposition, we feel offended. We sometimes transfer hurts of the past onto the current situation and so relive the past.

SOME OFFENCES ARE NEVER FORGIVEN

There is always the possibility that someone who offended us once will offend us again. They may be highly insensitive to our feelings and not even realise that their behaviour causes us hurt, or they may realise they cause hurt but simply be indifferent to us. They may interpret our apparent indifference to their behaviour as a sign of weakness and seek to bully us. As mentioned earlier, forgiveness does not mean the suspension of our critical faculties, so in such a situation we should quietly distance ourselves from that person.

Realistically, we are never going to be able to forgive fully some offences; it may simply be beyond our capacity. Similarly, there may be relationships that we, or the other party, do not wish to restore. This may be the case for a great variety of reasons. What we need to do is to acknowledge this reality with the other party or, if they do not wish this, just to ourselves. We should then recognise the level of forgiveness we are capable of, commit the whole affair to Jesus, and move on mentally and emotionally.

FORGIVENESS IN ST LUKE'S GOSPEL, WITH COMMENTARIES

LOVE FOR ENEMIES Lk. 6:27–35

'But I say to you that listen, love your enemies, do good to those who hate you, bless those who curse you, pray for those who abuse you. If anyone strikes you on the cheek, offer the other also; and from anyone who takes away your coat do not withhold even your shirt. Give to everyone who begs from you; and if anyone takes away your goods, do not ask for them again. Do to others, as you would have them do to you.

'If you love those who love you, what credit is that to you? For even sinners love those who love them. If you do good to those who do good to you, what credit is that to you? For even sinners do the same. If you lend to those from whom you hope to receive, what credit is that to you? Even sinners lend to sinners, to receive as much again. But love your enemies, do good, and lend, expecting nothing in return. Your reward will be great, and you will be children of the Most High; for he is kind to the ungrateful and the wicked.'

❋ COMMENTARY ❋

What Jesus is recommending here is an extremely proactive attitude towards those who offend us. He tells us not to let offence penetrate our hearts and upset our inner poise. When we are offended, we should immediately refuse to react negatively. We can turn things around by forgiving the offender and treating him with as much warmth as we can. Jesus is not expecting us to be impervious to hurt or to not feel the sting of an offence – he knows well the pain of offensive words and deeds – he is saying that we should see the broader picture and not allow ourselves become caught up in the emotions of the moment.

Jesus tells us that the 'Most High' acts towards the ungrateful with kindness and that we should do likewise and pull ourselves up out of the murky waters of human sensitivities. He is advising us to have almost instant forgetfulness and act as though the offender is more important to us, and more dearly loved, than he was before he hurt us. This seems not only to be an inhuman response but highly impractical: we are just not made like that and could not implement such a course of action. But Jesus knows clearly what the alternative is: becoming consumed by injured emotions and thoughts of self-pity and revenge. This path can only lead to retaliatory offending and further offences in return.

Coming from a basis of deep respect for ourselves,

Jesus wants us to make forgiveness our response to any offence and thus never allow our spiritual brotherhood to be ruptured.

LOVE FOR ENEMIES LK. 6:36 AND JUDGING OTHERS LK. 6:37–38

'Be merciful, just as your Father is merciful. Do not judge, and you will not be judged; do not condemn, and you will not be condemned. Forgive, and you will be forgiven; give, and it will be given to you. A good measure, pressed down, shaken together, running over, will be put into your lap; for the measure you give will be the measure you get back.'

❋ COMMENTARY ❋

Jesus encourages us to forgive as he forgives. Jesus does not allow offence to sever the link between him and us; he does not retire from us and leave us unloved. Instead, he draws nearer to us and forgives us. He does not act towards us as we acted towards him; he repays offence with kindness and generosity. By doing this, he breaks the cycle of offence and counter-offence, and offers us warmth and acceptance instead. By following his example, we can lift ourselves up towards spiritual freedom.

If we have forgiven in the past, we will know from our own experience the affect it has on our psychological state. We feel unburdened; a wound that was persistently open begins to heal; we are no longer dominated by recurring negative feelings that depress our spirits. If we wish to receive we should give, if we wish to be forgiven we should forgive. The truth of forgiveness is so counter-intuitive that most of us never truly embrace it. We rarely ponder the paradox that forgiveness is for long enough to begin to allow its deep significance to enter our being. Yet this is what Jesus tells us we must do; the solution to our suffering lies in reaching out to those who offend us with non-judgemental acceptance. There is no other way to a healthy spiritual and psychological life.

A SINFUL WOMAN FORGIVEN LK. 7:36–48

One of the Pharisees asked Jesus to eat with him, and he went into the Pharisee's house and took his place at the table. And a woman in the city, who was a sinner, having learned that he was eating in the Pharisee's house, brought an alabaster jar of ointment. She stood behind him at his feet, weeping, and began to bathe his feet with her tears and to dry them with her hair. Then she continued kissing his feet and anointing them with the ointment.

Now when the Pharisee who had invited him saw it, he said to himself, 'If this man were a prophet, he would have known who and what kind of woman this is who is touching him – that she is a sinner.' Jesus spoke up and said to him, 'Simon, I have something to say to you.'

'Teacher,' he replied, 'speak. A certain creditor had two

debtors; one owed five hundred denarii, and the other fifty. When they could not pay, he cancelled the debts for both of them. Now which of them will love him more?'

Simon answered, 'I suppose the one for whom he cancelled the greater debt.'

And Jesus said to him, 'You have judged rightly.'

Then turning towards the woman, he said to Simon, 'Do you see this woman? I entered your house; you gave me no water for my feet, but she has bathed my feet with her tears and dried them with her hair. You gave me no kiss, but from the time I came in she has not stopped kissing my feet. You did not anoint my head with oil, but she has anointed my feet with ointment. Therefore, I tell you, her sins, which were many, have been forgiven; hence she has shown great love. But the one to whom little is forgiven, loves little.'

Then he said to her, 'Your sins are forgiven.'

✷ COMMENTARY ✷

Not all offences can be forgiven. We should gently and quietly distance ourselves from offenders who we find it beyond our capacity to forgive. But when we do forgive someone who hurts us then we are opening a channel of deep love between that person and us. We are stretching ourselves, pushing our boundaries out to cradle them in the warmth of our understanding and compassion. The natural instinct would be that the greater the offence the more likely we should be to pull back from any further risk of hurt. But by moving out in forgiveness we are saying to that person that there is no need for them to feel threatened or at risk, for we have not taken offence; we understand them and empathise with them. By acting in this way we offer that person the opportunity of engaging with us in a deeper love than had existed before they offended us. This is Jesus' way: the greater the offence the greater the love. This love necessitates the full application of our intellect as well as our hearts.

When we have a clear understanding of, as well as warmth of heart for, the offender, we can honestly act with forgiveness. He wants us to be motivated by real compassion; he wants total commitment; he is unmoved by mediocrity. He is critical of Simon and spells out clearly why. Simon was polite and hospitable but he showed no signs of love for Jesus. Mary, on the other hand, was wholehearted and demonstrable in her love, despite, or because of, her many faults. So let us rise to this demanding challenge and respond to those who offend us with a forgiveness that is filled with wisdom.

THE PARABLE OF THE PRODIGAL SON AND HIS BROTHER LK. 15:11–32

Then Jesus said, 'There was a man who had two sons. The younger of them said to his father, "Father, give me the share of the property that will belong to me." So he divided his property between them. A few days later the younger son gathered all he had and travelled to a distant country, and there he squandered his property in dissolute living. When he had spent everything, a severe famine took place throughout that country, and he began to be in need. So he went and hired himself out to one of the citizens of that country, who sent him to his fields to feed the pigs. He would gladly have filled himself with the pods that the pigs were eating; and no one gave him anything. But when he came to himself he said, "How many of my father's hired hands have bread enough to spare, but here I am dying of hunger! I will get up and go to my father, and I will say to him, 'Father, I have sinned against heaven and before you; I am no longer worthy to be called your son; treat me like one of your hired hands.'" So he set off and went to his father. But while he was still far off, his father saw him and was filled with compassion; he ran and put his arms around him and kissed him. Then the son said to him, "Father, I have sinned against heaven and before you; I am no longer worthy to be called your son." But the father said to his slaves, "Quickly, bring out a robe – the best one – and put it on him; put a ring on his finger and sandals on his feet. And get the fatted calf and kill it, and let us eat and celebrate; for this son of mine was dead and is alive again; he was lost and is found!" And they began to celebrate.

'Now his elder son was in the field; and when he came and approached the house, he heard music and dancing. He called one of the slaves and asked what was going on.

He replied, "Your brother has come, and your father has killed the fatted calf, because he has got him back safe and sound." He became angry then and refused to go in. His father came out and began to plead with him. But he answered his father, "Listen! For all these years I have been working like a slave for you, and I have never disobeyed your command; yet you have never given me even a young goat so that I might celebrate with my friends. But when this son of yours came back, who has devoured your property with prostitutes, you killed the fatted calf for him!" Then the father said to him, "Son, you are always with me, and all that is mine is yours. But we had to celebrate and rejoice, because this brother of yours was dead and has come to life; he was lost and has been found.'"

❋ COMMENTARY ❋

The father fully understands his younger son's motivation when he offended him, and although he forgives him, nevertheless he does not reinstate any inheritance. He is a wise man and reassures his other son that there will be no change to his entitlement. Jesus is telling us that we should never suspend rationality when we forgive: in fact, we should apply it more thoroughly than ever.

Through forgiveness, we reach beyond the offender's behaviour while maintaining our own inner peace, poise and intellectual integrity. We do not desire to be reassured by the offender nor do we have any emotional dependence on them. The reward we experience is solely the happiness of knowing that we have not closed the door on our fellow travellers in this world; secure in God's love we are open to them and will never, regardless of what they do, reject them or treat them as strangers. Jesus never has low standards and in the case of forgiveness, the demands on us are enormous. For this reason forgiveness probably is, from the spiritual perspective, the most beneficial activity we can engage in. If an offender realises the hurt he has caused and asks for forgiveness then we may experience a new level of happiness. This was the joy the father of the prodigal son experienced when he saw his son returning. We do not set out with such consolation as our goal but gratefully accept it if it comes.

SOME SAYINGS OF JESUS LK. 17:3–4

'Be on your guard! If another disciple sins, you must rebuke the offender, and if there is repentance, you must forgive. And if the same person sins against you seven times a day, and turns back to you seven times and says, "I repent", you must forgive.'

✳ COMMENTARY ✳

For Jesus, forgiveness is not a once-off affair; it is something to be repeated over and over again. It is not that he is advocating continual subjection to offence – the point he is making is that forgiveness is a practice. He is emphasising that by repetition we make forgiveness part of our make-up. We want to have freedom of spirit and to live in the here-and-now, and not to allow offences, either present or past, to colour our relationships with those with whom we interact.

In real terms, if we do not practise forgiveness in the small encounters of everyday relationships, we are unlikely to be willing or able to do so when major problems arise. In our human relationships, we need to make forgiveness part of our whole awareness. Forgiveness is a fundamental tenet of spirituality. Through it, we are purged of emotions and attitudes that are serious blocks to the development of our spiritual lives.

THE CRUCIFIXION OF JESUS LK. 23:33–34

When they came to the place that is called The Scull, they crucified Jesus there with the criminals, one on his right and one on his left. Then Jesus said, 'Father, forgive them; for they do not know what they are doing.'

❋ COMMENTARY ❋

Often people offend us out of total ignorance. They simply do not see or comprehend the link between their actions and our being hurt. The reasons for their blindness may be many and complex and almost impossible to understand. We find it hard to forgive someone who walks away from us without any acknowledgement of how they have offended us. Yet this is what Jesus did; he was crucified by people who thought he deserved it. In their eyes, he was a dangerous man who was leading innocent people astray. Such levels of ignorance are hard to comprehend let alone forgive. But before Jesus died he expressed his unconditional forgiveness. Not only did he forgive them, but he was filled with compassion for them. Let our hearts direct us to feel as Jesus felt and with deep compassion for those who offend us, reach out to them in forgiveness.

∞ 4 ∞

PEACE

When the conscious mind transcends the subtlest level of thought, it transcends the subtlest state of relative experience and arrives at the transcendental Being, the state of pure consciousness or self-awareness.

Maharishi Mahesh Yogi

❧ INTRODUCTION ❧

We are all looking for a release from the demands of every-day life. We feel somewhere in our inner selves that life is not just about hectic action. We intuitively feel the need for peace. Certainly, we have to engage with life and develop our skills in order to survive. But we know that these concerns do not constitute the whole of life's responsibilities. We need to look beyond the active side of life and bring the experience of stillness into our lives. Peace was central to Jesus' message to his disciples. His early life with Mary and Joseph was lived quietly and peacefully. He constantly gave his blessing of peace to the people that he cured. If we wish to progress spiritually, we need to practise the art of deep relaxation, which brings us in contact with our spiritual nature.

PEACE

All life is made up of activity and rest. From plant life to animal life and onto human life, a basic cycle of activity and rest is followed. We know instinctively that we need both aspects to have a balanced life. In today's busy world the scales are all too often tipped in favour of activity, leaving us deficient in rest. Although sleep provides us with physical and mental rest we also need a rest that punctuates our daily activity. We need to have a type of rest that allows the mind to reduce its activities and allows our thoughts to become less constant. This automatically happens when our bodies experience the deep restfulness of meditation. It is in this state of profound rest that we are most open to the spiritual dimension of our lives and can best communicate with Jesus.

Unfortunately the world we live in has, to a great extent, lost the understanding and experience of this meditative rest and has become more and more dominated by activity. We used to have six days of activity and rest on the seventh day. But now, Sunday has become as busy a day as all the rest, with shopping from dawn to dusk. Even our leisure time is highly planned and filled with activities of all sorts. Our children have little opportunity to explore their own imaginations as every moment is structured. We cannot keep up a life of endless activity. Physically, our bodies demand rest and psychologically, our minds need escape from the constant strain of concentration. When activity is all we experience we start to define ourselves in terms of what we do and not in terms of who we are. We do this because our whole emotional and psychological world has grown to know nothing other than activity. We have lost contact with the intuitive reflective side of our life and hence relate only to the active side. When we know only activity, then inevitably we define rest as the absence of activity. We have no first hand knowledge of peacefulness and consequently cannot talk of it as an independent part of our lives. But when we have an intimate knowledge of peace we know it in its own right and define life as a balance between peace and activity, with neither dominating. Peace is seen as enriching activity and activity is seen as enhancing peace.

Jesus constantly withdrew to quiet places to give time to the non-active side of life. He brought his disciples away into the mountains so they could learn from him how to be still. If we wish to follow Jesus, we too need to retire to the mountains.

Jesus advised us to be in the world but not of it. When we develop the reflective side of our lives through frequent periods of retiring from activity, we learn to maintain an awareness of quietness while engaged in activity. Throughout Jesus' active life, he was filled with this spirit of peace; he was never separated from it nor broke his communion with it. We too can learn never to become totally immersed in doing, but to carry with us an underlying experience of being. This is not to say that our attention may in some way become divided. When we are active, we are fully active; our minds are sharper and generally more alert and focused because we are so deeply rested. But we never become overtaken by the activity, it does not possess us. As soon as it is over our minds do not cling to it, we return to a state of tranquillity as the wave of mental activity dies down.

When we have a real and vibrant experience of peace, we begin to value it in its own right. We look forward to the time we put aside for quiet. We become familiar with the various shades and characteristics of the experience just as we are familiar with the active side of life. Jesus urges us to live life filled with peace, to make peace the hub around which the wheel of our life spins. He blessed his disciples with peace and encouraged them to bless others similarly. When we are constantly engaged in the active side of life we are continually exposed to the rough and tumble that interacting with others inevitably brings. But when we withdraw into quietness we disengage from this turbulent sea and are embraced by tranquillity. It is in this silence that we move closer to ourselves and Jesus and experience the rest he promised. Our frayed emotions are soothed and healed and our over worked minds are re-energised.

MEDITATION, A PRACTICAL WAY
TO DEVELOP INNER PEACE

If we communicate with Jesus only through mental prayer, our receptiveness to inspiration coming from him is dulled as we tend to concentrate on what we want to convey. Whereas, when we still our minds and bring our bodies to a state of deep rest, we open ourselves to the spiritual side of our nature. We have moved beyond any intellectual activity into a profound experience that engages our whole being. In this state of rest, without distracting thoughts, our whole attention can turn to Jesus and we can hear with great clarity what he says. In the deep state of rest, we talk to Jesus without words. We commune with him through our very being and are as one with his spirit.

If we wish to develop this state of communion with Jesus then firstly we need to engage ourselves in a practice that will help us still our minds and relax our bodies. Meditation has traditionally been used to great effect in quietening the activities of the mind and body. In the past, the importance of silence in the spiritual life was better understood, and consequently time was given to engage in the practice of meditation. But today we are more likely to read about the value of peace and silence rather than to experience it. Even our churches, which used to be places of silence, are putting more and more emphasis on the social side of religion. Regularly, on entering an empty church for some prayer, we find that piped music is there to greet us, probably designed to fill our emptiness!

What will follow in the next section are suggested ways to practise relaxation. Once we have begun to do this we will be better disposed to a deeper and more profound quality of prayer.

This suggested programme has as its basis extracts from the gospels in which Jesus discusses peace. By reflecting on Jesus' peaceful spirit we can be convinced that giving time to experience peace is not only good for our health generally but is essential for spiritual development.

There are various practices that can help us reduce our physiological activity: physical exercises, yoga, breathing exercises, smell or sight concentrations, meditations. Centres which offer instruction in these practices are available throughout the world and may be found locally or sourced on the internet. One practice, which has proven to be particularly helpful in achieving this goal, is Transcendental Meditation, introduced to the west by the Hindu monk, Maharishi Mahesh Yogi. The basis for this practice is a word or mantra that we recite repeatedly. Our minds gently focus on the mantra and slowly other thoughts begin to slip away until the mantra is eventually left alone. In parallel with this reduction in our mental activity is a reduction in our physical activity. Our heartbeat slows and our breathing gets progressively shallower. At a certain stage, we reach a point where the mantra itself ceases and we are left with an experience of pure awareness. We have no thoughts whatsoever, yet we remain fully conscious of our surroundings. We can introduce a thought and contemplate or reject it. We are in control of our minds rather than our minds continually feeding us with random thoughts. The experience we have is one of great freedom, peace and happiness. We need nothing to occupy us for we are fully occupied.

In this state, we can then turn our hearts to Jesus and welcome him. By simply saying his name, we are filled with his presence for there is nothing else competing for our attention. We have cleared our bodies and minds of everything that might distract us and have opened the door to him. Jesus' spirit merges with ours until we cannot tell the difference between the two. This is a vibrant experience of Jesus that has nothing to do with thinking about an experience of Jesus. The two are very different. One is mood-making the other is a real-life encounter. To think about the experience of his presence would be to view Jesus from an outside and removed position. To experience Jesus is a dynamic, lively encounter that engages our whole being in a totally present and spontaneous way. This is the experience of oneness that Jesus talked about. This is the experience he prayed to his father that we might enjoy, just as he enjoys with his father: oneness without any sense of him and us; a communion where the only experience is of unity.

If we believe in transubstantiation, the changing of bread and wine into the body and blood of Christ, then receiving communion should be a most profound experience of union with Jesus. But very often we are so physically distracted that we barely register his coming. We need to realise the fine balance between our physical and spiritual lives, and relax our bodies before we receive communion. Essentially, we cannot welcome Jesus into our lives if at the same time we are being distracted by other stimuli. If, on the other hand, we have first brought ourselves into a deep experience of peace, then on receiving communion we almost immediately have an awareness of Jesus in us. Our senses are highly tuned and our whole consciousness is bathed in this deep union. Jesus is with us and we are with Jesus; we need nothing else. It is for this that we came into the world and this is where we hope to go after we leave it.

This experience is not just for saints and the holy, it is for all of us, without exception. In the past we lost the understanding, and hence the practice, of stilling our minds and relaxing our bodies, and grew to believe that Jesus' words had no practical application in our normal everyday lives. As a result of this, we accepted pious words and discussions about inner peace and unity, without any hope or belief that we might experience it. This led to our spiritual lives becoming very dry and formalised. This is not what Jesus taught his disciples. He offered the living reality of himself that all could spiritually touch and see. We, today, are fortunate that this experience is once again understood and that it is there for us, just as Jesus wanted it to be.

❧ THE PROGRAMME ❧

Here is a programme that we might follow to develop inner peace. The programme has two steps: meditating on peace in St Matthew's and St John's gospels, and practising meditation.

STEP ONE: MEDITATING ON PEACE IN ST MATTHEW'S AND ST JOHN'S GOSPELS

Find a relaxed time during the day to read over some of the extracts where Jesus refers to peace (see p. 109). You will see how peace was the very essence of Jesus and how often he wished peace on those he met. Allow these passages to inspire you to take up a practice that will relax you both physically and mentally and help you be more open spiritually.

STEP TWO: PRACTISING MEDITATION

As mentioned earlier, the practice of Transcendental Meditation, or TM, has been found to be highly effective in reducing activity in the mind and body. This practice relaxes us, leaving us disposed to experiencing spiritual realities. Those who are interested in this practice can make contact with teachers of TM who will fully introduce them to all that is involved in learning to practise TM.

Repeating this extract from Psalm 46:10 is a practice that may help us to relax and make contact with our inner selves:

Be still and know that I am God.

No matter what practice we choose, some general guidelines will be helpful. We should find a quiet place where we can be on our own for at least fifteen minutes, undisturbed. This can be a church, or a room at home, or a quiet place outdoors. We should make ourselves as comfortable as we can and perhaps have a candle burning if we are indoors. We should also wear something warm, as our body temperature will reduce as we quieten down. We should then close our eyes and slowly begin repeating our chosen word or phrase. We should be aware that our objective is to reduce the flow of thoughts and therefore should not engage in pondering on the meaning of what we are repeating. Inevitably, thoughts will rise up uninvited so we should gently let them come and go. We should not strain to repress them but bring our attention back to repeating our phrase as soon as we become conscious of these thoughts.

Getting a balance in our daily lives between activity and rest very much depends on each individual's circumstances but as a general rule we should aim to have a period either in the morning or evening when we can be alone. Ideally, we should have both periods but, for many, that can prove difficult. In the past people went on a retreat at least once a year. It was an extremely valuable practice for it allowed them to have an extended time for more in-depth meditation. Today, good places to revive this practice are retreat centres and monasteries. Monasteries in particular are highly aware of the stress and strain of modern-day living and are only too willing to provide facilities for those who wish to retreat and experience peace. In monasteries, not only do we have plenty of quiet time to ourselves, but we can take inspiration from seeing monks living a life dedicated to prayer and contemplation.

BE STILL AND KNOW THAT I AM GOD

TM may be viewed as a secular practice that aims to dispose us to the experience of the spiritual, but for some, a more obviously christian slant might be more suitable. To this end, the phrase 'Be still and know that I am God', can be helpful. We should, however, be aware that the initial objective is a physical one: to calm ourselves. Once we have calmed ourselves we will be disposed to experiencing the spiritual on a profound level. If we have not succeeded in quietening our minds to a meaningful degree, then we are likely to be too distracted to be open to the spirit. One difficulty at this early stage is that we may be inclined to reflect on the meaning of the words we are repeating, i.e. to think about Jesus. This is a real obstacle to the objective of relaxing. We need to relax first and then introduce thoughts of Jesus, not the other way around.

THE PULL OF ACTIVITY

The experience of deep peace inevitably gives way to the return of thoughts and the desire to engage in action. While we have a body we cannot avoid this pull back to the world of form. When we die and leave this world and no longer have a body, then we suspect things will be different. But while we are in this world we will always swing between the spiritual and the material. The benefit of the experience of deep peace in our everyday lives is that when we return to activity we bring with us a sense of that peace. We feel a new depth to our activity and a sense that we are never totally taken over by activity. Some people feel the inward pull towards reflection so strongly that they can minimise the active side of their lives and devote large portions of their day to reflection. But for most of us the most beneficial lifestyle is one that is highly active but allows us time for reflection as well.

SIMPLICITY OF THE PRACTICE

Nothing could be more natural or simple than the practice of deep rest. It is so easy that we may sometimes feel it too simple to be of any benefit. We live in a world that emphasises hard work as the means to reward and this contributes to our feeling that where there is no effort there can be no benefit. The notion that there is gain without pain is foreign. But in the practice of reflection this is exactly the case: the less effort, the deeper the level of peace. This is one of the great paradoxes associated with spiritual realities. It is not by our own effort that we grow, but by doing less and trusting Jesus more. Little children are more at home with this than those who are intelligent and analytical.

PEACE IN ST MATTHEW'S AND ST JOHN'S GOSPELS, WITH COMMENTARIES

THE MISSION OF THE TWELVE
MT. 10:11–14

'Whatever town or village you enter, find out who in it is worthy, and stay there until you leave. As you enter the house, greet it. If the house is worthy, let your peace come upon it; but if it is not worthy, let your peace return to you. If anyone will not welcome you or listen to your words, shake off the dust from your feet as you leave that house or town.'

✸ COMMENTARY ✸

It is possible that the apostles had already developed inner peace to a degree that it became intrinsic to who they were. When Jesus advises them to take their peace back if the household they enter does not deserve it, he is saying that they should put a high value on the peace they experience. They should judge whether the people they meet are responsive or not. A person who is peaceful can sometimes be regarded by others as passive or impractical and out of touch with the real world. They are sometimes treated with disdain and easily passed over. Jesus advises his apostles to have respect for themselves and not allow the preciousness of what they possess to be trampled underfoot. Today, in our highly active world, peace may not be held in too high a regard especially by those whose whole lives are dominated by action. In the workplace, for example, we may be satisfied with our position and not put ourselves forward for promotion so that we have a less stressful life and spend more time with our family and friends. This may be seen as lacking ambition to some. If we are in the company of such people, we should do as Jesus recommends and move on.

JESUS THANKS HIS FATHER MT. 11:28–30

'Come to me, all you that are weary and are carrying heavy burdens, and I will give you rest. Take my yoke upon you, and learn from me; for I am gentle and humble in heart, and you will find rest for your souls. For my yoke is easy, and my burden is light.'

✳ COMMENTARY ✳

Sometimes we find the burden of life difficult to carry. Maybe we are suffering from ill health in body or mind, or someone close to us is in pain. We may have persistent problems with our relationships or have financial problems or worries about aspects of our lives. The weight of these difficulties may cause us to lose sleep, to be generally irritable, or to avoid interaction with people. Burdens are often felt more deeply if we think we can never free our minds or bodies of them. We cannot get a break from the strain and our lives become one long endurance test. If we could get some temporary relief, we would be better able to shoulder the burden. Jesus is there listening. He understands and wants to help. He wants to give us rest. If we only truly believed this, we could be saved so much pain, especially in matters of paralysing worry.

If we trusted Jesus and went to him asking for his compassion we could relax and find peace in the confidence that the future will be better. Jesus has promised he will help us. We need to take him at his word and believe in our hearts that he cares and will not let us down. We can allow ourselves to smile and begin to stop worrying. When we are in the grip of worries, it is much more difficult to practise relaxation. If we travel the road with Jesus, nothing will be too onerous for us as he is always there. This has immense practical implications. Let us trust Jesus and go to him for it is there we will find rest for our souls.

Prompted by her mother, she said, 'Give me the head of John the Baptist here on a platter.'

The head was brought on a platter and given to the girl, who brought it to her mother. His disciples came and took the body and buried it; then they went and told Jesus ...

Now when Jesus heard this, he withdrew from there in a boat to a deserted place by himself.

❈ Commentary ❈

When we receive bad news or when we reach a crisis in our lives, it is good to retire so that we can rest and reflect. If we meditate and still our minds, we give ourselves an opportunity to see things in a different light. We never return to a problem with the same attitude after we experience the deep rest associated with meditation. Often problems that seemed insurmountable before we meditated appear solvable after we meditate.

Philosophers, artists, creative business people, to mention a few, have found that after normal sleep they are more inspired. To be objective about a problem we need to have inner space where we can go and reflect from a broader perspective. This is what Jesus planned to do when he heard about John's death: to withdraw to a deserted place. No doubt, he was upset and wanted to have time to pray for John, to heal his own wounds and be inspired about the future. Too often, instead of doing what Jesus did, we choose to numb our pain through the anaesthetic of activity. We would rather not listen to our inner voice's directives. We fail to turn to Jesus in the stillness of our hearts and ask him to direct us. Let us resolve in the future to respond to life's challenges, not from any narrow vision, but from the depths of inner peace.

THE PROMISE OF THE HOLY SPIRIT
JN. 14:27

'Peace I leave with you; my peace I give to you. I do not give to you as the world gives. Do not let your hearts be troubled and do not let them be afraid.'

※ COMMENTARY ※

Jesus valued peace so highly that he made it his gift to his disciples. He could have given them wisdom or some other virtue but instead he left them the experience of inner peace. Peace is the bedrock of all spiritual experience. It is the deep stillness of the ocean upon which the waves of life rise and fall. Without peace, there can be no happiness, no fulfilment, no security, for we are living on nervous energy and have nowhere to go to draw fresh supplies of energy. Activity and effort cannot answer all our needs. There are things that are beyond their sphere of influence. Jesus has said that he gives us his own peace. How generous and compassionate this is. He knows our exhausted state and reaches out to us. We need to respond to him by learning to still our minds and bodies and thus leave ourselves open to the experience of his peace.

PEACE FOR THE DISCIPLES JN. 16:33

'I have said this to you, so that in me you may have peace. In the world you face persecution. But take courage; I have conquered the world!'

✸ COMMENTARY ✸

Inner peace gives us a certain ability to withstand the disturbing events of life. Because we have a peaceful inner life, we tend not to panic when things go wrong, nor do we fret over what negativity might befall us in the future. We have a calm that allows us to view things from a broader perspective and keep our hearts and minds free from worry. Without this inner peace, worry can drive us to try harder and harder to achieve until our lives becomes perpetual activity.

Jesus tells us that to live in this world is to have difficulties of varying degrees of seriousness. We cannot avoid them. But he also tells us that troubles need not possess our spirit and dominate our inner lives; he will give us refuge in his peace.

Jesus Appears to the Disciples
Jn. 20:19–21

When it was evening on that day, the first day of the week, and the doors of the house where the disciples had met were locked for fear of the Jews, Jesus came and stood among them and said, 'Peace be with you.' After he said this, he showed them his hands and his side. Then the disciples rejoiced when they saw the Lord. Jesus said to them again, 'Peace be with you.'

※ COMMENTARY ※

No matter what emotion we are experiencing at any given time, peace can be our refuge. We may be depressed and unable to lift ourselves, or we may be elated with adrenaline causing us to feel giddy with excitement. Either extreme of emotion leaves our spirits disturbed, agitated, with a feeling of expectancy. Deep inner peace is an experience of complete contentment; we feel no desire for any other stimulation. Unlike any other experience which would inevitably have its focus on the future or on the past, we look nowhere else but are completely in the present.

Jesus appeared to the disciples when they were in a state of great fear. They had bolted the door, no doubt wondering whether they were the next to be taken away and killed. Jesus knew they were afraid and calls them away from their fear to inner peace. Equally, he calls them away from their ecstasy, when they realise that it is he. Peace is the experience he wanted them to have and not to bob like corks on the unpredictable sea of human emotions. We need to realise the consistency of inner peace and the inconsistency of our emotions. Then we need to centre our lives on the consistent rather than the inconsistent.

∞ 5 ∞

ANGELS

Then the devil left him, and suddenly the angels came and waited on him.

Matthew 4:11

✎ INTRODUCTION ✎

In the gospels, the actions of angels are continually recorded. Usually they perform the role of messengers, either bringing good news or warning of danger. We also hear how they gave support, comfort and advice to people; often with great gentleness when they saw that their appearance was causing fear.

As human beings, we are familiar with most living creatures that inhabit our planet, but as spiritual beings we are less familiar with the entities that inhabit the spiritual dimension. This is because the spiritual world is, by definition, non-material and therefore not open to perception by our physical senses. To meet angels, we have to perceive them spiritually and, as with all spiritual matters, we have to start from the basis of faith. If we are christians, we have the gospel accounts of angels as a basis for our reaching out in faith. We can feel confident that we will be rewarded if we open our hearts to communicate with the angels that St Matthew tells us looked after Jesus when he was tired and hungry in the wilderness.

Angels, particularly guardian angels, have a real and active interest in our welfare. Guardian angels join us when we are born and stay with us until we die. They guide, protect, advise and love us as true friends. Our concerns are their concerns; our pains are their pains; our triumphs are their triumphs. Friends lift us up when we are feeling down, and cool our ardour when we are losing control of ourselves. Guardian angels are such friends also. It is well worth our while investing our time to get to know them.

OUR GUARDIAN ANGEL

Developing a relationship with our guardian angel is essentially like developing any other authentic relationship: it must spring from love. We must want to spend time talking with them, getting to know them, learning to trust them. We need to be sensitive, honest and have a sense of humour. We must be willing to reveal to them our innermost feelings and frustrations and not be afraid to express annoyance or disappointment if we feel let down by them.

Guardian angels are beings from the non-material world, who are assigned to us by the divinity to accompany us throughout our lives. Because they do not possess physical bodies, we can only know they exist, firstly through faith, and then through our own personal experience. Our guardian angel is our companion who is always close by and is willing to assist us across a whole range of issues. This assistance tends to be concerned with practical, everyday issues, rather than with the major issues in our lives. Initially, we may not be conscious of their interventions, but as our relationship with them develops and we actively ask their assistance, we become increasingly aware of their helping hand. As we grow to know our guardian angels, we begin to rely on them more and more and turn to them in a great variety of situations. They are always there when we need help: physical or emotional. They become so close to us that we talk to them in an informal manner: the language we use is simple, direct and unselfconscious. We are talking with someone who knows us so well they rarely have to hear the end of a sentence to know our needs. When we are irritated and aggravated by something or someone we tend to tell our guardian angel about it in an uncensored language. Our relationship is essentially intimate and light, casual and familiar.

We should not view our guardian angel as a fix-all agent whom we use day and night without any sense of the fact that we are indebted to them. They have free will, but by their very nature, they are infinitely generous and willingly put themselves at our continual disposal. We should be deeply grateful for such thoughtfulness and caring and never take our guardian angels for granted. If we realise that we are engaging in a real and vibrant relationship we will treat our guardian angel with respect and dignity. They are gentle and kind and this implies a certain sensitivity, so we need to be careful that we do not offend them. If we love as Jesus does, we will naturally treat our guardian angel as we should wish them to treat us.

❧ THE PROGRAMME ❧

When we make a decision that we want to develop an open, friendly relationship with our guardian angel, we can follow this suggested programme. This programme comprises two steps: meditating briefly on angels in the gospels; and dedicating a day to getting to know our guardian angel.

STEP ONE: MEDITATING BRIEFLY ON ANGELS IN THE GOSPELS

Pick any day in which you will be going about your normal activities, but preferably not one that you anticipate will be very busy. Start the programme in the morning by reflecting on passages from the gospels that deal with angels (see p. 131). The purpose of these reflections is to establish in your mind the basis for your faith in the existence of angels. Quietly read these selected passages until you become comfortable with the reality of angels, in the full knowledge that your faith in them is solidly based on the gospel. You need to feel a deep sense of inner ease with the actuality of angels before you commence your day, otherwise your desire to develop a relationship with your guardian angel is likely to be driven by superstitious fascination rather than faith.

STEP TWO: DEDICATING A DAY TO GETTING TO KNOW YOUR GUARDIAN ANGEL

If we have little experience of communicating with our guardian angel, then we may feel a little awkward addressing him as suggested below. But like all new encounters the initial stages are the most uncomfortable. Once we have embarked on this unusual dialogue and begun to get an intuitive sense of what our guardian angel is like, then that which once felt strange becomes familiar and comforting.

MORNING

Once you have finished your reflections you can then move onto a short prayer dedicated to your guardian angel. The suggested prayer below is the well-known, traditional one:

Angel of God my guardian dear,
to whom God's love commits me here.
Ever this day be at my side, to light,
to guard, to rule and guide.
Amen.

You can now address your guardian angel by saying to him that you wish to get to know him as a true friend. Tell him you know he has been at your side all your life caring for you and you are deeply appreciative and grateful for his love. Today you want to make this a two-way relationship where you talk openly and freely to him. Acknowledge that he is the one doing all the helping and you are the recipient, but when you meet in heaven maybe you will be in a position to repay him.

First things first, you need to address him by his name and, as you do not know his name, you had better give him one (unless he whispers it in your ear). Pick a name that you are comfortable with, inform him of it, and hope he will like it. Then tell him that you want to keep in touch casually and informally throughout the day, but that there is one thing you would like to request of him first. You would like to ask would he do something during the day that would show you that he is there, hearing you, and acknowledging this new beginning to your relationship? This can be anything at all – the simpler the better – something that you might normally consider fortuitous or a happy coincidence but that you will now feel is his hand at work. You can ask him to do something specific or leave it to him to decide.

AFTERNOON

The more you develop a trust that is firmly grounded in the gospels, the more you will intuitively know you are truly communicating with your guardian angel. As the day progresses you should talk to him, ask his advice, help and protection, as you would your closest friend.

There should be no strain in any of your communications with your guardian angel; you should be completely relaxed. You should not even feel that you are doing something different. You should simply be going about your normal daily life except that now you are doing a little more 'internal' talking. You are not trying to achieve anything; you are just getting to know someone. You have many other relationships and responsibilities in your life and the last thing your guardian angel wants is for you to see him as a burden. He will be quite happy if you ignore him for long periods if you are overstretched. He will not love you any less and, in fact, will be there at your side even more attentively.

EVENING

When the evening comes, you can review the day and, if you feel good about it, you can tell your guardian angel how much you enjoyed his company. You can also see if something happened during the day that you knew involved his intervention. If he did something for you, you should thank him from your heart and tell him you look forward to a long and enjoyable friendship. If things did not go as you hoped, you can either complain to him or wait to see if there is a bigger picture. He may have held off to allow something else to happen. If you feel he did not do anything for you, then you can ask him to make amends the next day. You should believe that he will intervene and, with great trust, you should not be afraid to push him.

There is a deeper level to your asking your guardian angel to communicate demonstratively with you, albeit in the simplest of ways: by asking for his assistance on a regular, daily basis. By reaching out to him and sharing your feelings and thoughts, you will see that, just as the angels did in the gospel stories, your guardian angel will assist you and be there for you when you need him. As positive experiences mount up, you will grow in confidence and will find a spontaneous love welling up in your heart for your dear friend. As you finish this day and lie down to sleep, you should say goodnight to him.

PROTECTION

We are taught from an early age the importance of our guardian angel as our protector. The protector role they play is a central role in our lives, and probably saves us from dangers we will only learn of when we die. This should fill us with great warmth towards them. We might have considered ourselves just fortunate at the time of such an event, but now we are more likely to see that it was their hand that averted real tragedy. We should also reflect that when we were unfortunate to have events go very badly for us, it is possible things could have been much worse had it not been for our guardian angel's intervention.

Embarking on a journey, be it a long one or a short one, is always a good time to call on our guardian angel and ask them to keep us safe. We can also ask them to look over those dear to us if they are travelling or we can ask them to have a word with our loved ones' guardian angels and request them to be vigilant with their charges: guardian angels talk!

Ultimately, though, we are all destined, sooner or later, to depart this world. It follows, therefore, that even our guardian angels cannot, nor would they want to, protect us from this inevitability. So at some time in the future the protective shields that our guardian angels have around us will have to be lowered. We hope and expect that by that time we will be so eager to move on that we will hardly notice.

GENDER

Because angels are referred to in the gospels by gender-specific names, it could be assumed that there are both male and female angels. The problem is we do not know which gender our particular guardian angel is. Therefore, to move things forward, perhaps a good idea is to choose a name according to our own gender. We can tell our guardian angel that if we get his or her gender wrong, we will rectify the situation when we meet in the next life!

PADRE PIO AND GUARDIAN ANGELS

No contemporary christian account of angels would be complete without some reference to the relationship the now-canonised stigmatic, Padre Pio (an Italian Capuchin friar), shared with his guardian angel. From a very young age, Padre Pio both talked to and saw his guardian angel. He thought it quite normal to do this and was somewhat confused when he realised that others did not do likewise. For Padre Pio, his guardian angel was his childhood friend. This relationship remained right up until his death, and we can only assume that it continued even after that. Padre Pio related to his guardian angel across the full range of human emotions. He trusted him implicitly and seemed to share his every hope and fear with him. For us today who are eager to develop a deep and intimate relationship with our guardian angel, we can do no better than reflect on this sublimely personable friendship. The book, *Send Me Your Guardian Angel*, by Fr Alessio Parente, Padre Pio's personal helper for many years, recounts stories about Padre Pio and his relationship with his guardian angel. In this book, we hear tales of guardian angels laughing, crying, sulking, knocking on doors, driving cars and, of course, protecting their charges. Here are two of many such stories.

The first, 'An angel laughs!', was recorded on 29 November 1911, and relates to Padre Pio talking to his guardian angel while in an ecstasy. Their relationship is clearly that of intimate friends who are relaxed and enjoy having fun. Padre Pio's words were feverishly transcribed by Fr Agostino of San Marco in Lamis:

> ... Angel of God, my Angel ... are you not taking care of me? ... Are you a creature of God? ... Either you're a creature of God or a creator ... You're a creator? No. Therefore you are God's creature and you have laws which you must obey ... You must stay beside me whether you want to or not ... he laughs ... what is there to laugh about? Tell me one thing ... you must tell me ... who was here yesterday morning? ... and he laughs ... you must tell me ... who was it? ... Either Father Agostino or the Superior ... tell me then ... was it perhaps their secretaries? Answer me

now ... If you don't answer me I will say it was one of these four ... he laughs ... an Angel laughs! ... Tell me then ... I won't leave you until you tell me ...

The second story, 'The busy angels', is Alessandro da Ripabottoni's story about Padre Pio, recounted in *Padre Pio da Petrelcina*, in which he, with great humour, shows his desire that others should believe in the reality of their guardian angels.

One morning, I was a little late and, afraid that I would not be in time for Padre Pio's Mass, I said: 'My guardian angel, go to Padre Pio and tell him to wait a little before celebrating; as a sign that you will do me this favour, lift off his scull-cap!' I hurried to the Friary and, arriving at the church, I saw Padre Pio in front of the altar steps, ready to begin the Mass. I attended the Mass, after which I went into the Sacristy and saw that Padre Pio was opening the cupboards in search of something. I said to him: 'Padre, what are you looking for?' He replied: 'My son, I can't find my scull-cap anymore!' I remembered then what I had said to my guardian angel so I told Padre Pio. He looked at me in a manner which said, 'Now you believe it?' He started to look for the scull-cap again and finally, he found it in his hood.

ANGELS IN THE GOSPELS, WITH COMMENTARIES

THE BIRTH OF JESUS FORETOLD
LK. 1:26–38

In the sixth month the angel Gabriel was sent by God to a town in Galilee called Nazareth, to a virgin engaged to a man whose name was Joseph, of the house of David. The virgin's name was Mary. And he came to her and said, 'Greetings, favoured one! The Lord is with you.' But she was much perplexed by his words and pondered what sort of greeting this might be.

The angel said to her, 'Do not be afraid, Mary, for you have found favour with God. And now, you will conceive in your womb and bear a son, and you will name him Jesus. He will be great, and will be called the Son of the Most High, and the Lord God will give to him the throne of his ancestor David. He will reign over the house of Jacob for ever, and of his kingdom there will be no end.' Mary said to the angel, 'How can this be, since I am a virgin?' The angel said to her, 'The Holy Spirit will come upon you, and the power of the Most High will overshadow you; therefore the child to be born will be holy; he will be called Son of God. And now, your relative Elizabeth in her old age has also conceived a son; and this is the sixth month for her who was said to be barren. For nothing will be impossible with God.' Then Mary said, 'Here I am, the servant of the Lord; let it be with me according to your word.' And the angel departed from her.

❋ COMMENTARY ❋

This is a very intimate and detailed exchange between Mary and Gabriel. How highly valued and trusted Gabriel must be in the sight of God; he is the one chosen to deliver this cosmic-shaping, humanity-changing news. How delicate and sensitive Gabriel is in his approach to Mary. He knows she is terrified, highly confused and bewildered. What he has to tell her is almost beyond belief and he knows she will need every drop of courage and faith to hear it. Gabriel conveys his message clearly and accurately, and we can imagine that his tone is soft and his tempo unrushed, and his body language relaxed and supportive.

This account tells us so much about the nature of angels: about their power and majesty, their gentleness and caring, but above all, about their love for us. We should have no fear of venturing out from behind the wall of the familiar and reaching out with a sense of adventure to our guardian angel.

THE TEMPTATION OF JESUS
MT. 4:1–2, MT. 4:11

Then Jesus was led up by the Spirit into the wilderness to be tempted by the devil. He fasted for forty days and forty nights, and afterwards he was famished …

Then the devil left him, and suddenly angels came and waited on him.

❈ COMMENTARY ❈

Angels are so close to, and trusted by, Jesus that he drops all defences and gives himself over to their care. The Highest of the High entrusts himself to these spiritual beings. Angels must indeed be very special beings worthy of our greatest trust and confidence. Let us not doubt for a minute their existence and, with eager and friendly arms, open our minds and hearts to their great love.

THE RESURRECTION OF JESUS MT. 28:1–8

After the sabbath, as the first day of the week was dawning, Mary Magdalene and the other Mary went to see the tomb. And suddenly there was a great earthquake; for an angel of the Lord, descending from heaven, came and rolled back the stone and sat on it. His appearance was like lightning, and his clothing white as snow. For fear of him the guards shook and became like dead men. But the angel said to the women, 'Do not be afraid; I know that you are looking for Jesus who was crucified. He is not here; for he has been raised, as he said. Come, see the place where he lay. Then go quickly and tell his disciples, "He has been raised from the dead, and indeed he is going ahead of you to Galilee; there you will see him." This is my message for you.' So they left the tomb quickly with fear and great joy, and ran to tell his disciples.

❈ COMMENTARY ❈

See how tenderly this angel behaves towards the two Marys? He realises they are shocked at seeing him and he immediately wants to reassure them and allow them to regain their composure. He is gentle and kind, and yet we can almost feel his power and authority. His face was like lightning, which implies a commanding presence and strength. How terrified the unfortunate guards were; never before had they encountered anyone like this. This angel is portrayed doing what angels do so often in gospel stories: delivering an important message. Let us try to open our ears so that we might become sensitive to the messages our guardian angels are relaying to us.

∞ **6** ∞

DEATH

Jesus, I trust in You

St Maria Faustina

INTRODUCTION

Death, which brings about the cessation of the physical world, inevitably comes to us all. On a particular day at a particular time our everyday experiences of the world we have been born into and have grown up in, come to an abrupt end. We lose contact forever with all the experiences we have been fed by our senses. We can no longer smell flowers in spring, touch the warm hands of the ones we love, see the beauty of a sunrise, hear the music of the masters or taste the rich flavours of foods. All these things will be no more for us. But we are not solely physical beings, we are also spiritual beings. We have the ability to reason and to reflect, a capacity for intuitive knowing, and an awareness of the unity of others and ourselves on the deepest level. Jesus tells us that these spiritual attributes survive physical death. We, as spiritual beings, continue to exist beyond death with no break in continuity. In a very real sense, we wake from the slumber of life in the physical world to the experience of the fully vibrant life of the spiritual. Jesus tells us of this transformation and urges us to prepare for it now while we are still in this physical world. If we truly realise the reality of this, it makes sense for us to resolve to do all we can now to develop our spiritual life and not live only with an eye for material existence.

END OF PHYSICAL EXISTENCE

At death, with the cessation of all activities, relationships and physical involvements, we leave the chessboard of life without ever being able to make another move. Dramatically and finally, we cut all attachments that we formed and maintained. Perhaps most shockingly of all, we cut our relationship with our own physical bodies. We are no longer the male or female person of such an appearance or age or social circumstance. That composition of water and matter, that particular atomic arrangement that we had grown to know as us, no longer exists. We have to leave our bodies behind and bid them farewell. We must leave unfinished all businesses, projects and ventures that we had been engaged in. All emotional attachments to those we love can no longer be fed by personal contact and must, on the physical level, be let go. The effect of such severance on our spirits is monumental. Never in all our lives have we experienced such a fundamental shaking.

Often the finality of death hits us only when we are brought into close proximity with it, for example when someone dear to us dies. We tend not to address death in any meaningful way until that moment. When we are inevitably confronted, we begin to ask questions about its meaning; but intellectual questions about death invariably yield few answers. Ultimately, it is only when we turn our attention to the meaning of life, as seen from the perspective of death, that we gain insight. When Jesus was asked how to reach the goal of existence, he gave two great directives: love God and love your neighbour. These encapsulate the meaning of all existence – both in this life and the next. By following this path, we are initiated into the experience of the unity of all creation. We begin to rethink our attitude to the world and we embark on a quest to find a balance between our physical and spiritual lives, while we still have time.

We cannot carry into the next life anything physical or material; Jesus tells us all we take with us are the qualities of our character and our spiritual nature. It inevitably follows that if we have done our best to nurture the spiritual in our lives then when we die we will have a familiarity with the next world (of which the essential nature is spiritual). On the other hand, if we have clung to the material side of life then we will be at sea in the next life. One of the main reasons we experience pain in the next world is because that world is a non-material, non-sensory one and if we have only identified with these aspects in our world then the loss is painful. We have allowed ourselves to develop a taste for that which does not last, and when our time here is up, we are left with an attachment, a craving, for that which we can never experience again. Thus, it follows that the decisions we make now shape the type of experience we will have after death.

Jesus' two great directives can guide us towards experiences that will promote the spiritual quality of our lives. If we live life according to these, then when it is time for us to leave this world we will do so with little fuss. It will be as natural for us as it is for the caterpillar when he sheds his cocoon in order to spread his wings and fly. Our lives will have been lived to a substantial degree on the spiritual plane and our attachment to the things we experience through the medium of our bodies will have much less hold over us.

DEVELOPING AN AWARENESS OF DEATH

By developing an awareness of death and by living our lives in the knowledge of its certainty, we encourage ourselves, as Jesus advised, to stay awake and not allow ourselves to become sedated by the transitory things of this world. What follows below are four observations and, in the next section, a programme that may help us do this. The observations concern aspects of death for us to reflect on. The programme is based on a visualisation exercise and a set of questions that will help us focus on our preparedness for death. This will be supported by meditations on relevant passages from St Mark's Gospel (p. 149).

Observations

First observation: All things must pass

All things come to an end and are followed by new beginnings. In our physical world, we see this process taking place continually: the long hot days of summer end as autumn winds begin to blow; the sun sets and the moon rises. In our personal relationships, we see this cycle in motion: childhood friendships are often superseded by teenage ones; old business acquaintances lose energy and meaning when new projects begin to emerge. Our own fortunes follow this pattern: we have lean periods followed by periods of plenty; high status from which we suddenly fall.

If we look back on the past, we can see figures who commanded respect and wielded power who today are given cursory acknowledgement in history books. Graveyards have many grandiose, highly decorated headstones to people we know nothing about today. By reflecting on this transitory nature of all life, we begin to accept that we are part of this cycle – not outside or removed from it. The more this becomes part of our fundamental attitude the more at ease we will be with the reality of our own ultimate end.

Second observation:
Get comfortable with death

We need to be comfortable with our own impending death. We should be aware that, as for every other creature on this earth, death is never very far away. If we spend some time with those who are coming to the end of their lives – be it in the material, personal or physical spheres – then this reality will be brought home to us. If, for example, we visit nursing homes or spend time with those who are dying, we will be confronted by the reality of death very dramatically. Such experiences will help us to grow in empathy and unity with all humanity. We will grow in the awareness of the fundamental truth that nothing physical lasts forever.

By doing even very simple things that take us outside the normal comforts we enjoy in life, we will experience a lessening of our attachment to those comforts. This will help us to distance ourselves now, while we live, from the things that we will have to leave forever one day. We should choose to experience things that bring us down from our protected castles so that we can walk on our feet of clay.

THIRD OBSERVATION:
DEATH IS PASSAGE TO UNION

When our physical death takes place, we pass into a world of pure spiritual experience. Death is not the end but the passage through which we pass on our way to this new dimension. Jesus defeated death by rising, and when asked about the resurrection he replied that he was the resurrection. From this, we learn all we need to know about the afterlife. Union with Jesus through love *is* the afterlife. By learning to love Jesus and those with whom we live our lives here on earth, we are already entering into this union. When we die, Jesus will bring us into total and complete union with himself and all creation for all time.

FOURTH OBSERVATION: LOVE

By developing love in our hearts, we draw closer to our ultimate goal of unity with one another and with God. The degree to which we develop love in this life is the degree to which we will experience it after death for it is here on earth that we develop our capacity to love. If we live a life predominantly directed towards self-gratification then we will have no experience or ability to accept Jesus' love when he greets us after we die. We will turn away from his love because we will not be able to embrace it; we will simply want to run to the sensory experiences that we spent our lives immersed in, and have grown so accustomed to, and comfortable with.

Death teaches us to value the love we share now, to focus on it, to prioritise it and not let the cares of this world cloud it. All too often, we give our hearts over to worry, and neglect love. We spend more time planning our lives than living them. Our minds are so full of other concerns that we cannot see we are missing the very purpose of our existence: to love. When we are with our loved ones but let our minds be elsewhere then we are not truly present. We act as though life will continue to give us years without end and there will be plenty of time later to love. We do not realise that now is the time to love with a sense of deep gratitude and tenderness. Now we are here, tomorrow we may not be.

If we learn to trust Jesus more and worry less, we will be more disposed to prioritising love. We need to trust that Jesus will provide for us in this world and will be there to greet us in the next. Inspired with this confidence we can then live happily, sharing love. We need to see this bigger picture of love and make it part of our awareness so that our lives become centred on the principle of love. While we are here on this earth, we have the opportunity to expand our hearts, to grow in empathy and compassion for others and infuse our whole being with a caring love. But when we die we are cut off from further physical contacts with others – our time is up. We need to bring the reality of the shortness of our time here to our conscious minds.

Jesus asked the question: what does it profit us if we succeed magnificently in this world if it all turns, in such a short time, to dust. We need to ponder this and direct our lives away from short-term gains when they distract us from our real purpose of growing in love.

✌ THE PROGRAMME ✌

Here is a programme we could follow to develop an awareness of death in our daily lives. The programme has two
steps: meditating on death in St Mark's Gospel; and practising visualising our death.

STEP ONE: MEDITATING ON
DEATH IN ST MARK'S GOSPEL

Quietly and gently read the extracts from the gospel in
which Jesus discusses death (see p.153). Do not concentrate too strongly on what you read for you are about to
become engaged in a demanding exercise. Simply be content to be reassured by Jesus' soothing words.

STEP TWO: PRACTISING THE
VISUALISATION OF YOUR DEATH

The purpose of this visualisation exercise is to assist you
in developing a general awareness of death. By becoming
aware that your physical life is passing, you will be encouraged to invest your energies in that which survives death:
your spiritual life. St Ignatius of Loyola used similar practices in his *Spiritual Exercises*.

Decide on a time of day when you can lie down on your
bed and not be disturbed. It is best to select a time when

you are not tired so you do not fall asleep; an ideal time would be mid afternoon when the sun is still shining and nature is exuberant. Lie down, with perhaps a light blanket over you, and relax. Let your body and mind settle for a minute or two. Then slowly and quietly picture the following:

You are on your deathbed. Your physical health has deteriorated to the stage that you can no longer make any significant moves. Your breathing is shallow but still even. Your mind is clear but you are tired. You know you are approaching your end. You know that you shall soon be excluded from the life that is continuing to go on all around you. The birds are still singing and the bees are buzzing but, for you, activity has all but ceased. Your body feels heavier than it has ever done before, as though it did not belong to you. You swallow, smell the air and realise that these will be the last sensations of taste and smell that you ever have. You look around the room and wonder what aspect of it will be the last thing you ever see. As you listen to the sounds outside, you realise that these are the last sounds you will hear.

In this state, you can now ask yourself the following two sets of questions: the first set to help you ascertain the degree of your attachment to the physical world; the second set to help you ascertain how much you have loved and how spiritually ready you are for the afterlife. These are sample questions and not an exhaustive list. There may be other questions you want to add.

SET 1. PHYSICAL ATTACHMENT:

- Are you uncomfortable with leaving this physical world and entering the wholly spiritual world?
- Do you feel a strong pull back towards the possessions you have and the ambitions you have not fulfilled?
- Do you feel a desire to stay in your body and not be denied sensory experiences?
- Do you feel fear of the unknown or a quiet expectancy of entering the familiar?
- Do you regret leaving loved ones?

SET 2. LOVE IN YOUR PERSONAL RELATIONSHIPS:

- Did you extend yourself and show empathy and compassion towards others?
- Did you forgive?
- Did you help?
- Was your heart open, free and welcoming?
- Did you love your family, friends and others?
- Did you spend time in reflection and giving your heart to Jesus?
- Did you feel Jesus was a friend or someone you did not really know?
- Did you love Jesus?

After you have asked these questions and given ample time to allow the answers to seep into your heart, you can stand up. Experience again the vitality and energy that fills your body. Perhaps wash your face in cold water and feel the freshness of life. Go to the window and look out at the world. Thank Jesus for the opportunity your life affords you. You are alive and can direct your energies to attaining whatever goal you desire. The choice is yours.

CONCLUSION

Our answers to these questions will inevitably not lean fully in one direction or the other. But we should be able to get a sense of where we can try harder to wean ourselves off the physical world and stir ourselves more passionately to embrace the love that will lead us to union with Jesus in the next life.

DEATH IN ST MARK'S GOSPEL, WITH COMMENTARIES

JESUS FORETELLS HIS DEATH AND RESURRECTION MK. 8:34–9:1

He called the crowd with his disciples, and said to them, 'If any want to become my followers, let them deny themselves and take up their cross and follow me. For those who want to save their life will lose it, and those who lose their life for my sake, and for the sake of the gospel, will save it. For what will it profit them to gain the whole world and forfeit their life? Indeed, what can they give in return for their life? Those who are ashamed of me and of my words in this adulterous and sinful generation, of them the Son of Man will also be ashamed when he comes in the glory of his Father with the holy angels.' And he said to them, 'Truly I tell you, there are some standing here who will not taste death until they see that the kingdom of God has come with power.'

✻ COMMENTARY ✻

Jesus is saying that to follow him means living in this physical world with all its distractions and attractions of both mind and body. We must somehow cope with it all and find our way through the things that drain our spirits and sap our resolve. We must be tough. Weaning ourselves off the physical delights of this world and developing a taste for spiritual realities is not easy. We need to take our eyes off trying to gain the world. We need to let go of heady ambitions, desires for status, privileges and prestige, and all the other things that we cannot take with us when we die. What good are they? Jesus asks this repeatedly.

Can we imagine standing in front of Jesus listening to his every word when all of a sudden he says that there are some standing there who will not taste death before they see the kingdom of God? Imagine the tingle that would run down our spines if he scanned his audience and his gaze fell on us.

THE TRANSFIGURATION MK. 9:2–6

Six days later, Jesus took with him Peter and James and John, and led them up a high mountain apart, by themselves. And he was transfigured before them, and his clothes became dazzling white, such as no one on earth could bleach them. And there appeared to them Elijah with Moses, who were talking with Jesus. Then Peter said to Jesus, 'Rabbi, it is good for us to be here; let us make three dwellings, one for you, one for Moses, and one for Elijah.' He did not know what to say, for they were terrified.

❋ COMMENTARY ❋

We can be so used to, and familiar with, this earthy existence that we become foolhardy and brazen and think we know all there is to know. We can fall so completely into patterns of behaviour and thinking that we become complacent. But this physical existence is certainly not all there is to creation; we know so little about what else is out there. No doubt, Peter, James and John were like us and, with a certain complacency, believed they were going for yet another trip into the wilderness for reflection and private dialogue with Jesus. What a shock it must have been. Indeed, we are told they were terrified when Jesus blazed with overwhelming radiance and whiteness. He moved way beyond anything they had ever experienced and they were left speechless. Poor Peter was the first to try to make some sense of what was happening and, of course, he got it all wrong.

This scene should fill us with volumes of hope as we struggle through this life. Think of it, try to imagine that one fine day when we have to go through what inevitably will be the unsettling experience of dying, we will have as consolation the knowledge that Jesus will shortly greet us and bring us into a powerful and stunningly beautiful new existence. The best is yet to come.

The Death of Jesus Mk. 15:33–34

When it was noon, darkness came over the whole land until three in the afternoon. At three o'clock Jesus cried out with a loud voice, 'Eloi, Eloi, lema sabachthani?' which means, 'My God, my God, why have you forsaken me?'

❋ Commentary ❋

When it is our time to die, the circumstances may influence the ease with which we leave. Dying suddenly and unexpectedly may mean almost no experience, if any, of physical or mental pain. We may literally be dead before we know it. On the other hand, we may die after a long and difficult illness, having experienced great pain. If we die violently and unjustly and are aware of all that is happening, we may feel deeply abandoned and violated. If we die surrounded by loved ones and have reached old age, we may feel great gratitude and contentment. We cannot know what the circumstances surrounding our deaths will be and consequently we cannot prepare for them.

What we can do now is trust Jesus, knowing that he will be close at hand no matter what happens. Even if we feel total despair and aloneness, we should hold onto hope with a grip of steel. No matter how extreme the circumstances may be, we should never allow ourselves to be robbed of hope in Jesus.

Ponder now and instil this hope into our beings, so that

it is part of our mental and emotional lives. Above all, take consolation and draw courage from the last words of Jesus, the master of life and death: 'My God, my God, why have you forsaken me?' If he could feel this, we should fear nothing.

THE RESURRECTION OF JESUS MK. 16:1–8

When the sabbath was over, Mary Magdalene, and Mary the mother of James, and Salome bought spices, so that they might go and anoint him. And very early on the first day of the week, when the sun had risen, they went to the tomb. They had been saying to one another, 'Who will roll away the stone for us from the entrance to the tomb?'

When they looked up, they saw that the stone, which was very large, had already been rolled back. As they entered the tomb, they saw a young man, dressed in a white robe, sitting on the right side; and they were alarmed. But he said to them, 'Do not be alarmed; you are looking for Jesus of Nazareth, who was crucified. He has been raised; he is not here. Look, there is the place they laid him. But go, tell his disciples and Peter that he is going ahead of you to Galilee; there you will see him, just as he told you.' So they went out and fled from the tomb, for terror and amazement had seized them; and they said nothing to anyone, for they were afraid.

✳ COMMENTARY ✳

These three women were still full of love for Jesus even though he seemed not to have lived up to the promises he had made to them. He had promised to be their strength and protector and always be there for them. The apostles were in hiding, confused and in fear for their lives. These women were not going to abandon Jesus; they were going to do things that expressed their gentle and tender warmth for him. The men stayed behind locked doors, but for these women, love overcame fear and out they ventured. Picture the scene: it was early morning and the sun was just rising. Although they did not realise it, it was the perfect setting for a monumental new beginning. They were full of the practicalities of human love: who will roll away the stone? Once they saw the young man inside, everything changed, not just for them, but for all of us, forever. For christians, Jesus is the bridge between earthly life and the life beyond. Take him out of the picture and we should all be like the two Marys and Salome: warm-hearted but lost. Jesus is our guide. Where would we be without him? It is extremely difficult to make sense of this earthly existence, but can we begin to even imagine how impossible it would be to navigate the next world without Jesus' compassionate and infinitely wise love? What is important is that Jesus is there watching over us. We can afford to relax and allow ourselves be human: to make mistakes, to be foolish, to be confused, to be scared out of our wits. Jesus is the resurrection; that is, he is love. Love is now and love is then. That is all we need to know; that is all there is to know. Jesus eagerly and earnestly wants us to open ourselves to him as completely as we can in this world. Then, in the next world, our union with him can be made complete.

REFERENCES

Dalai Lama, *The Good Heart: His Holiness the Dalai Lama Explores the Heart of Christianity – and of Humanity* (London: Rider, *1996).*

Di Lella, Alexander, *OFM et al* (translators), *The Holy Bible.* N.R.S.V. Catholic Edition, Anglicised Text (London: Darton, Longman and Todd, 2005).

Fustina, St Maria, *Come to my Mercy: the Desires and Promises of the Merciful Saviour as Recorded in the Diary of Saint Maria Faustina, booklet, arranged and introduced by Rev. George W. Kosicki, CSB (*Massachusetts: Marian Press, 1994).

Loyola, St Ignatius, *The Spiritual Exercises of St Ignatius Loyola, English edition, translated by Thomas Corbishley, SJ (*Hertfordshire: Anthony Clarke, 1973).

Maharishi Mahesh Yogi, *The Science of Being and Art of Living, fourth edition (*London: International SRM Publications, 1967).

Parente, Fr Alessio, *OFM CAP (*ed.), *Send Me Your Guardian Angel,* third edition (Our Lady of Grace Capuchin Friary, Foggia, 1997).

Pio, Padre, *'Efficacious Novena to the Sacred Heart of Jesus',* in *Blessed Padre Pio of Pietrelcina Capuchin, pamphlet (*Our Lady of Grace Capuchin Friary, Foggia, 1971).

Pio, Padre, *In My Own Words, compiled and edited by Anthony F. Chiffolo (*London: Hodder and Stoughton, 2001).

Teresa, Mother, *Love, Joy and Peace* (London: Harper Collins Religious, 1998).

Transcendental Meditation (TM) website: www.tm.org.